I SAW THE
WORLD END

I SAW THE WORLD END

An Introduction to the Bible's Apocalyptic Literature

William C. Nicholas, Jr.

Fr. William C Nichols

12-12-07

Paulist Press
New York/Mahwah, NJ

Cover design by Sharyn Banks
Book design by Lynn Else

Library of Congress Cataloging-in-Publication Data

Nicholas, William C.
    I saw the world end : an introduction to the Bible's apocalyptic literature / William C. Nicholas, Jr.
        p. cm.
    Includes bibliographical references and index.
    ISBN 978-0-8091-4450-1 (alk. paper)
    1. Apocalyptic literature—History and criticism. I. Title.
    BS646.N53 2007
    220'.046—dc22

                                                                    2007006250

Published by Paulist Press
997 Macarthur Boulevard
Mahwah, New Jersey 07430

www.paulistpress.com

Printed and bound in the
United States of America

"About that day and hour no one knows, neither the angels of heaven, nor the Son, but only the Father."

—Matthew 24:36; Mark 13:32

"It is not for you to know the times or periods that the Father has set by his own authority." —Acts 1:7

"I tell you, my friends, do not fear those who kill the body, and after that can do nothing more." —Luke 12:4

CONTENTS

INTRODUCTION

Throughout the history of Christianity many events have been accompanied by expectation of the world's end and the second coming of Christ. During the first Christian century many expected Jesus to return soon, within their lifetimes, and saw the very act of spreading the gospel as indicating that the end was near. As the church began to experience persecution at the hands of the Roman Empire and the generation that witnessed Christ's life began to die, Christian understanding of end-time events began to adjust.

As the Roman Empire in the West fell to barbarian tribes and the law and order of now Christian Rome began to collapse, many within the empire saw the events as ushering in the final culmination of the kingdom of God and the end of the kingdom on earth. Others, including the church, saw an opportunity to spread the gospel to these new invaders from beyond the empire.

Many saw the outbreak of the Black Death in fourteenth-century Europe as a plague of apocalyptic proportions because of the high death rate, the contagious nature of the disease, and the outward appearance that God had abandoned them to the pandemic. Still others saw the plague not as an apocalyptic end, but as a call and an opportunity to express the love of God through the care many gave to the sick, dying, and dead at the risk, and often the expense, of their own health and lives.

As the world trudged through the Cold War in the decades following World War II, the fear of nuclear annihilation drew many religious groups to equate the end of the world with nuclear holocaust. When the nation of Israel was established in 1948, thus beginning an ongoing conflict with the Arab nations in the region, many saw it as the event that would usher in the beginning of the end. When the Cold War ended many thoughts turned to China or

Arabia as the source of the great enemy whose war against Christianity would usher in the parousia.

As the new millennium approached and the world grew closer to the year AD 2000, some, particularly in religious circles, again turned their minds to the idea of the end times. Some focused on the end of the world, others on the coming of Christ, still others on some great catastrophe that would affect the world as a whole. For a large portion of the computer-using world, this expectation, either directly or indirectly, took the form of a concern over the Y2K bug, which many believed would affect the world's computers and throw the general infrastructure, including financial and defense systems, into a flurry. Other concerns were of possible terrorist threats, which some feared might spark a great war between world powers. This would result in widespread bloodshed, destruction, disease, and a deterioration of law and order into worldwide anarchy and chaos. In anticipation of these possible events, some began to stockpile water, food, and weapons so as to be ready for whatever onslaught would accompany the great shift from the second to the third millenniums.

The turn of the millennium has come and gone, with no related cosmic or social catastrophe to speak of. That has not prevented apocalyptic interest from continuing within the church and society. With the terrorist attack against the United States on September 11, 2001, and the lingering threat of atomic attack, fears regarding a catastrophe of "apocalyptic" proportions have weighed on people's minds. With the continuing war on terror in Arab-Muslim countries, many have speculated on the reality of a global war with devastating consequences. With the popularity of the *Left Behind* novels and the recent release of the cinematic remake of *The Omen* (on 6-6-06, no less), popular interest in apocalyptic prophecy regarding the anti-Christ and the end of time continues to flourish.

Throughout these various periods in history, and in our own time, there has been a persistent interest in certain books of Holy Scripture that have traditionally dealt with the end times—particularly the Books of Revelation and Daniel. While some groups interpreted the events of Scripture in literal, often fanatical ways—as a blueprint for the end of the world—others have sought simply to familiarize themselves with what the books present and the messages they seek to communicate.

While many have put aside immediate fears concerning the end of the world, some groups continue in their efforts to recalculate the exact time when the world will end and when the second coming will occur. Commercially it has become key to tapping into a cultural zeitgeist in order to profit from a popular fascination with the mystery of how all things will end. On the whole, however, it has become the stuff of nightmares on one hand, of Christian triumphalism on the other, and a source of confusion for some who seek to reconcile the fearsome judge depicted in apocalyptic scenarios with faith in a loving, forgiving God who has saved us.

For the rest of us, however, for whom apocalyptic literature is still a part of inspired Scripture, curiosity in the books dealing with the end times continues to linger, as does a desire to understand better the part these books play in the tradition of the inspired word of God. Seeking to grow beyond the popular, fearsome, often commercial approaches, many sincerely desire to learn how the Books of Daniel and Revelation fit into the overall good news of Jesus the Christ. What does apocalyptic literature mean to people of faith? How does it play into the day-to-day lives of people who live that faith? How is it relevant to people who seek to understand more fully the faith they profess?

Throughout my years of study in the seminary I have read a number of books on Scripture, both as required texts and as extra reading. This has continued during my ministry since ordination to the priesthood. Many of these works approached Scripture with an in-depth exegetical study. In parish work, however, I have found that the average Catholic is less interested in heavy academic approaches to Scripture, and more interested in how it speaks to him or her both personally and as a member of the church. Catholics in the pews, admiring such scholars as Raymond Brown, understand that Catholic biblical study is at times complicated and recognize that heavy exegesis is valuable. Nevertheless, they seek guidance in making the message of Scripture more real and more tangible to them.

Therefore, with regard to apocalyptic writings, if the end of the world can never be known, how are we to understand biblical apocalyptic literature? If the message of Scripture, particularly the New Testament, is essentially good news, how does the Book of Revelation play into our faith as Christians? Since we read from the Book of Revelation so infrequently in our Sunday liturgy (only eight times during a three-year cycle), and the Book of Daniel even less frequently, how important are these books as part of our inspired Scripture?

What I have sought to do in this short study is present an explanation of apocalyptic literature. This is no straightforward task. My structure and approach is based in part on parish Bible studies I have offered. I present and review various biblical and extrabiblical apocalyptic writings, as well as the principal apocalyptic books of the Bible—Daniel and Revelation. While I make use of exegesis—indeed with apocalyptic literature it is quite necessary—it is not my principal focus or thrust. While I include explanations stemming from exegetical study I do so only to enhance my presentation of the message within the books. I do not focus on an in-depth, word-for-word, verse-by-verse interpretation. Rather I seek to present the overall story (or stories), passages, or images, and explain them in ordinary language to ordinary parishioners—as ordinary, that is, as a study on apocalyptic literature can be.

Study questions are provided at the end of each chapter. The questions in Roman type are intended to assist you in processing and discussing the material; questions in italics are reflective questions to help you relate the material to your own faith life.

If one is to study Scripture responsibly, one cannot understand fully the message for today without understanding the historical context from which it came. Such understanding does not hinder, but rather enhances the manner in which Scripture speaks to us today. Therefore, in order to grasp the message of Revelation or Daniel, indeed any book of Scripture, it is necessary to understand the message for the people of that particular period. As inspired Scripture, however, it has a message that is universal to people of faith in all times and places. Much of what I present focuses on this history—on what was happening to the Jews or to the Christians at the time the books were written. This also includes a cultural context, which at times takes into account some of the pagan mythologies of the era.

Introduction

Whereas many of the books I have read include a reprinting of the Books of Daniel and Revelation, I do not do so here. I quote various passages from throughout the Bible, but I do not reprint entire books as part of this study. While I take most of my quotations of Scripture from the New Revised Standard Version of the Bible, I do not seek to present a "more accurate translation" as part of this study. Nor is this book meant to replace one's reading of Sacred Scripture. It is my hope, rather, to enhance your own reading of the Bible, whatever translation or edition you may have in your home. Therefore, I have presented this study in such a way as to hope that as you read it, the Holy Bible is nearby and open to the appropriate book and passage.

1
AN INTRODUCTION TO APOCALYPTIC LITERATURE

WHAT DO WE MEAN BY "APOCALYPTIC" LITERATURE?

The word *apocalyptic* describes the literature of the Books of Daniel and Revelation. It is taken from the Greek word *apocalyptein*, which means to pull back a veil or to uncover. This "uncovering" can also be understood as making known something that previously was unknown. Hence, the term *apocalyptic* can be understood as serving to uncover, or *reveal*, something unknown or hidden.

At the time the Book of Revelation was written, the word *apocalypse* was used to refer to written works concerning revelation itself. As scholarship developed, the term *apocalyptic* came to be used to describe a type of literature and its characteristics. One such work is the Book of Daniel, found among the Prophets in the Old Testament. Today, *apocalyptic* is defined as referring to something of, relating to, or resembling an apocalypse. A volume on apocalyptic literature, *Semeia* 14, published in 1979, discusses all forms of apocalyptic literature from various ancient civilizations. The compiled definition of apocalyptic literature contains a number of specific characteristics:

> A genre of revelatory literature with a narrative framework, in which a revelation is mediated by an otherworldly being to a human recipient, disclosing a transcendent reality which is both temporal insofar as it envisages eschatological salvation, and spatial insofar as it involves another, supernatural world.[1]

Consider each element of this definition. Apocalyptic is a genre or type of **revelatory literature**—it reveals something unknown. This can include, but is by no means limited to, something about the future. It is not, however, the same as literature that expresses or depicts dreams, visions, prophetic oracles, or a dying man's final testament.[2]

Apocalyptic literature reveals a **transcendent** reality. The essence of its message or story is beyond the here and now. This reality is **temporal**—that is, it envisions future eschatological salvation and reveals present otherworldly realities. It is also **spatial**—that is, it involves supernatural, otherworldly journeys, such as a tour of the heavenly realm, that reveal the interconnectedness between the heavenly world and the human world.

Apocalyptic literature is **narrative**—it tells a story with a universal focus. It is not of a personal nature. Thus, the Apocalypse of John found in the Book of Revelation is not intended solely for John or for the seven churches to which it is addressed, but is for the entire church. While the author writes or tells the story in the present time frame, the narrative often sets the story in the author's past. The story then catches up to the present and projects into the future (see Fig. 1).

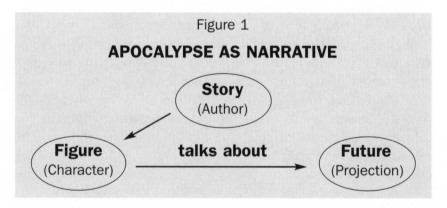

Figure 1

APOCALYPSE AS NARRATIVE

There is a **human recipient** of revelation given by a **heavenly being,** such as an angel, who serves as an interpreter of the heavenly vision. In the Book of Revelation, for example, during the vision of the vast multitude (Rev 7:13–14) one of the elders explains the meaning of the vision. Often the interpreter delivers a long, complex, symbolic discourse containing the revelation, and then explains it to the human recipient. These discourses often involve a real vision or a literary composition that draws on traditional literary language and symbolism. Hence, apocalyptic discourses need explanation and interpretation because they always involve symbolic language.

Using this narrative form, the author often connects the story with some important figure of the past. This figure serves as the human recipient of the vision, and his name is used as a pseudonym to add credibility to the revelation being offered. "John" of the Book of Revelation and "Daniel" of the Book of Daniel are two prime examples.

Apocalyptic texts in the Bible—Daniel and Revelation—were written during times of great crises, such as a persecution or conquest, with the purpose of renewing the people's faith that the universal reign of God is over and above the present reality. They emphasize an eschatological event brought about through divine intervention, which brings about a renewal and reordering of creation. The writing of apocalyptic works was intended to exhort or console the people in light of the particular situation so as to provide hope for the imminent downfall of the oppressor and the victory of the oppressed.[3]

As we will see in the following chapters, apocalyptic literature, especially in the Books of Daniel and Revelation, does not seek to answer questions regarding particular events of the future. Rather it looks to faith in the future—insofar as God's salvation is concerned—in order to give hope for the present. We have faith that God's future victory is assured. Therefore the victory whereby God saves us is spoken of in dynamic and uplifting ways so as to inspire renewed zeal and hope in light of the present situation. It serves more or less as an intense spiritual pep talk of sorts to inspire hope in the midst of persecution. The reality of persecution does not change the fact that all life and all creation are in motion toward God, and nothing will prevent its reaching its final destination, in God's good time.

APOCALYPTIC ESCHATOLOGY

What about "the End"?

"Apocalyptic" usually refers to either the collapse of the current social order, an upheaval in the natural or cosmic order, or—in a religious context—the end times.

Eschatology is a branch of theology that deals with the last things. The word comes from the Greek words *eschatos* (last things) and *ology* (talk) and was first used in 1804 to describe the last things on a personal level—that is, eschatology refers to death, purgatory, judgment, resurrection, heaven, and hell. When the Bible talks about the last things, however, it focuses not on the personal, but on the cosmic and the social. Biblical eschatology speaks of hope for a future in which our circumstances are changed in such a way as to speak of something entirely new. It describes the last things in terms of a final definitive goal for all things, rather than for one particular person. Hence, the end times are not understood in terms of the end of history or the end of the world, but rather its final goal—the ultimate purpose for which creation was created.

In short, the question of how much apocalyptic literature has to do with the end of the world can be answered in two words: not much! This does not, however, mean that apocalyptic literature does not focus on the end of all things—quite the contrary. Rather than focusing on the end in terms of how an existence comes to an end or how time comes to an end, apocalyptic literature speaks in terms of the ultimate goal and aim of creation.

It is important to note that for the cultures of the ancient Near East, the cosmos worked and moved in a cyclical fashion. The people remained passive, living and adjusting to the movement of the cosmos. The days came and went, the seasons changed, the death of the elderly was seen as related to the birth of the young, and the cycle repeated. The people learned to predict, adapt, and adjust to the cycle, from which came an understanding of the cosmos and its mastery over humanity. This led to religious beliefs in gods and goddesses who influenced the cosmos, in which the struggle of good against evil was also seen as cyclical. Cultic practices

4

developed as people sought to appease the cosmic forces that affected day-to-day life.

The Hebrew mindset, however, was unique among those of other ancient cultures. Their faith and spirituality developed to understand history and life as linear rather than cyclical. All creation begins with God (Alpha) and is in motion toward God, who is the ultimate end of all things (Omega). Therefore, the faith of the Hebrews was not one of human passivity, nor did they see God as aloof. Rather, they worshiped a God who was connected to the people, who had a relationship with them. The people enjoyed a covenant with Yahweh, to whom they offered worship.

As Christians we understand this end as the final manifestation of our salvation. Therefore, we can accurately claim that we are living in the midst of the end times, and have been for over two thousand years. This is because we are living in a world that God has made his dwelling place. After creating the world, God came to live within it, and redeemed it as part of the divine plan. Therefore, we live in a world in which the purpose of creation—salvation—has been fulfilled in Christ's death on the cross. All that remains to be fulfilled is the day when Christ will come again to usher in the final realization of the kingdom of God.

Where apocalyptic literature is concerned, the end—which is God—is spoken of in terms of the experience of the people of that period in history. The message, however, is universal, and therefore relevant to us today and to people of all time. While speaking of its eschatological hopes, apocalyptic literature seeks to answer the question: if all things move toward their ultimate end in God, then how do we understand our circumstances now?

Symbolic Language

Symbolic language is used throughout the Scriptures to express the meaning of things that are beyond conventional description. It speaks in terms of what is familiar to describe something that is unknown or to communicate extra meaning or depth to an experience.

> For dogs are all around me; a company of evildoers encircles me.   (Ps 22:16)

> As a deer longs for flowing streams, so my soul longs for you, O God.   (Ps 42:1)

The reality spoken of in eschatology defies conventional description. Therefore, eschatological language is always symbolic. No one can describe a firsthand experience of death, because no one has experienced it in such a way as to give an account. Neither can we describe the events surrounding the return of Christ, because it has not yet happened. Further, our limited intellect and vocabulary could not hope to do justice to the grandeur and glory of such an event. Therefore, we use symbols and metaphors.

Only images, metaphors, and symbols rooted in a deeper reality can catch the depth of both eschatological truth and the many aspects of our relationship with God. Symbols and symbolic language are filled with images.

> The path of the righteous is like the light of dawn, which shines brighter and brighter until full day.   (Prov 4:18)

> A shoot shall come out from the stump of Jesse, and a branch shall grow out of his roots.   (Isa 11:1)

An image is not meant to give a literal description of spiritual or eschatological truths—not what it is or will be, but rather what it is or will be *like*.

Biblical Eschatology

The Bible contains two different kinds of eschatology: prophetic and apocalyptic. Both come from a particular period in history and reflect the spiritual development of that particular time. While they address what the Hebrew people were experiencing at that particular time, they also reflect a universal development in faith and spirituality.

Prophetic eschatology calls upon Israel's past as it speaks about a definitive future in order to give hope for the present. In the early period of their history God led the Hebrew people through an exodus from Egypt, to a covenant on Mount Sinai, bringing them into the Promised Land. God blessed the dynasty of King David and inspired King Solomon to construct the Temple in Jerusalem. Later on, however, the people of Israel violated the covenant more and more. The kingdom eventually split in two, and the Davidic dynasty was in decline. Finally, the Israelites were faced with the destruction of the Temple and the Exile to Babylon. In the midst of this turmoil and the people's infidelity to the covenant, the prophets called the people to remember their glorious past before their infidelities, and to turn back to God so as to be the people and the kingdom they once were.

Prophetic eschatology remembers these past events, but speaks of the future of Israel as something "new" in this world. The prophets drew from the traditions and experiences of old to look to the future. Prophetic eschatology speaks of a new covenant written in the heart, a new David, a new kingdom, and a new Temple. Such expressions as the "Day of the Lord" and the "Day of Judgment" refer to a day in which the enemies of Israel will be judged and vanquished, and the New Israel will be brought about permanently.

Apocalyptic eschatology, on the other hand, has lost all hope in the present and in its vision for the future. There is no message for the present order. Therefore, apocalyptic eschatology calls for an end to the present world so as to bring about the new world. It is not aimed at changing behavior. Rather, it seeks to understand what is happening in the present and encourage hope for the future. So where prophetic eschatology focuses on this world and its history, apocalyptic eschatology focuses on another world, having lost hope in the present.

Apocalyptic eschatology claims that there is another world beyond or behind this one, a world of angels and demons, good and evil, a world in which all the real action takes place, of which action in this world is only a shadow. Since apocalyptic eschatology tends to regard God as absent from a mysterious world, we seek a revelation from the world beyond in order to give meaning to this world.

There is a strong conviction in apocalyptic eschatology that God is in control and has a definite purpose, even though we may not see or comprehend it. A revelation from beyond helps us to understand that purpose better. This adds to the confidence and triumphalism, often seen in apocalyptic literature, that God's plan will be carried out despite the struggle, persecution, and tragedy experienced by God's servants. In short, nothing can stop God's plan for our salvation, least of all pagan persecution. Therefore those undergoing persecution should strive to endure.

This does not mean, however, that strict determinism—the idea that everything is prescribed and that our life or our choices are made passively in the midst of a mechanically programmed course of events—is the principal thrust of apocalyptic eschatology. Rather, aspects of determinism (God's definite plan) are balanced with free will (do we choose to forsake that plan or not?). The inclusion of judgment, particularly in the Book of Revelation, indicates that free will is very much a part of the eschatological scenario. While God has a definite plan that will not be overcome, we are still free to accept or reject it, to endure struggle and persecution or give in—and are judged accordingly. If God's plan is being carried out, what do we do about it, how do we respond? If redemption has been accomplished in Christ's death and resurrection, how do we as people who are saved live our lives in view of that salvation?

Finally, apocalyptic eschatology is filled with dualisms—good versus evil, us versus them, the temporal versus the spatial, this world versus the next world, here versus there, God versus Satan. In the Book of Daniel, Daniel and the religion of Yahweh are pitted against Babylon and its pagan gods. In the Book of Revelation, it is Christ against Satan, the Lamb against the beast, Christianity against Rome.

Millenarianism

Later in this study we will read the passages that are relevant to the apocalyptic notion regarding the great millennium, also known as the thousand-year reign. However, due to modern eschatological ideas based on certain interpretations of symbolic language in biblical texts, there is much current speculation on the millennium, the end times, and the second coming of Christ.

Therefore, before we enter into the biblical texts, a few comments regarding the phenomenon known as millenarianism are in order.

Revelation 20:1–10 speaks of a period when the dragon, or Satan, will be confined for a thousand years. During this period Christ and the martyrs will reign. When the thousand years are over Satan will be released to make a final assault on the righteous before being destroyed once and for all (see the section on the thousand-year reign).

In addition to the Book of Revelation, there are a number of apocalyptic works that are not found in the Scriptures (see the following section on the Books of Enoch). In 2 Enoch 33:1–2, salvation history is summarized as a series of seven periods of a thousand years corresponding with the seven days of creation, with the eighth millennium being the end:

> On the 8th day I likewise appointed so that the 8th day might be the 1st, the first created of my week, and that it should revolve in the revolution of 7000; < | so that the 8000 | > might be in the beginning of a time not reckoned and unending, neither years, nor months, nor weeks, nor days, nor hours <like the first day of the week, so also the eighth day of the week might return continually>.
>
> (2 Enoch 33:1–2)[4]

While 2 Enoch is not included in the Bible, it nonetheless reflects an ancient mindset regarding periods of a thousand years. In this passage the millennia are spoken of as days of the week. For the author, each "day" represents a millennium. The eighth day is understood as the final millennium that will continue forever.[5]

Even the fathers of the church speak of periods of a thousand years before Christ's second coming. For example, St. Justin Martyr writes:

> I and every other completely orthodox Christian feel certain that there will be a resurrection of the flesh, followed by a thousand years in the rebuilt, embellished and enlarged city of Jerusalem. (Dialogue with Trypho, 80)[6]

This recurrence has led some to expect some manifestation of the end times with the turn of every thousand years of Christianity. This was more recently evident with the apprehension over the so-called Y2K bug at the coming of the year AD 2000 and the passage into the third millennium. While Y2K was more or less a concern regarding the continued function of computers and the defenses and services that depended on them, there were also expectations among certain groups of the second coming, of judgment, of parousia—or otherwise an end of some sort—with the turn of the millennium.

Be that as it may, reference to a reign of a thousand years appears only twice in the entire Bible; both are in the Book of Revelation and both occur in chapter 20.

> I also saw the souls of those who had been beheaded for their testimony to Jesus and for the word of God....They came to life and reigned with Christ a thousand years.
> (Rev 20:4)

> Blessed and holy are those who share in the first resurrection. Over these the second death has no power, but they will be priests of God and of Christ, and they will reign with him a thousand years.   (Rev 20:6)

There are two more references to a thousand years also found in Revelation 20. However, these passages speak of the period of Satan's confinement rather than the duration of a kingly reign.

> He seized the dragon, that ancient serpent, who is the Devil and Satan, and bound him for a thousand years.
> (Rev 20:2)

> When the thousand years are ended, Satan will be released from his prison and will come out to deceive the nations...in order to gather them for battle.
> (Rev 20:7–8)

Theologies, expectations, and apprehension regarding the millennium have grown to extreme proportions from these brief passages.

Throughout the history of Christianity many have taken these passages literally and have speculated on their meaning. Some suggest that the thousand years will be an earthly kingdom of peace. Others expect the millennial reign to occur after Christ returns, when he will reign for a thousand years before the final defeat of Satan and the end of time. Others have understood the millennium in a spiritual rather than historical sense. St. Augustine, for example, interpreted the binding of Satan to have been achieved in the life of Christ and the millennium to be the period of the church (*City of God*, 20).

There are, however, two prevailing interpretations of the millennium of the King of kings—literal and symbolic. The **literal approach** has in itself two main opinions as to when Christ will come in relation to the millennium. The premillennial opinion holds that Christ will come before the millennium. He will reign for a thousand years, after which will come the new heaven and the new earth.

The postmillennial interpretation believes that Christ will come after the millennium, that the world throughout history will gradually improve, making ready for the coming of the reign of Christ. Hence the apprehension as the year 2000 approached. This has been associated with the expectation of the great rapture and tribulation, which some American non-Catholic denominations have drawn out of 1 Thessalonians 4:13–17 as well as from the Gospels (Matt 24; Mark 13:5–37; Luke 21:5–36). They believe that the rapture will occur at the end of the millennium, when certain select people will be snatched up to heaven so as to escape the tribulation to follow. After this, Christ will come.[7]

It must be noted, however, that the ideas of rapture and tribulation are not Catholic terms, nor do Catholics adhere to a literal interpretation of the millennium. The Catholic Church has occasionally condemned the literal interpretation of the thousand-year reign. For example, the Fifth Lateran Council in 1516, in response to Reformation apocalypticism, discouraged preachers from predicting of the end of the world. Such activity was considered a detriment to the church's message.

[Preachers] are in no way to presume to preach or declare a fixed time for future evils, the coming of antichrist or the precise day of judgment….Let it be known that those who have hitherto dared to declare such things are liars, and that because of them not a little authority has been taken away from those who preach the truth.

We are placing a restriction on each and all of the said clerics, secular and regular and others, of whatever status, rank or order, who undertake this task. In their public sermons they are not to keep on predicting some future events as based on the sacred writings, nor presume to declare that they know them from the holy Spirit or from divine revelation, nor that strange and empty predictions are matters which must be firmly asserted or held in some other way. (Fifth Lateran Council, Section 11 [On How To Preach])

More recently Pope John Paul II, addressing a general audience on April 22, 1998, stated that attempts to predict the end of the world are "deceptive and misleading."

The other approach to interpreting the millennium, one more in line with Catholic faith, is the **symbolic approach**. The number of years is not taken literally, as there is no literal meaning. Rather, it is to be understood as a great number of years. This is in accordance with the nature of apocalyptic literature, and a similar number symbolism is seen in the Books of Daniel and Ezekiel. Even Psalm 90:4 states, "a thousand years in your sight are like yesterday when it is past, or like a watch in the night." Other books of the Bible, including Revelation, play with the symbolism of the number 1,000 to indicate a great number of soldiers, horses, treasures, and so on.

For St. Augustine, the heavenly victory encompassed in the history of the church is symbolized in a thousand years of victory, measured against the years symbolic of the church's suffering—three-and-a-half years. To those suffering persecution this would emphasize the insignificant time allotted to persecution compared to the astronomical length of victory for those who hold fast to faith. In that vein, another opinion is that the martyrs spoken of in the Book of Revelation are seen as already sharing in the victory of Christ. The thousand years symbolize the period between the resurrection of the martyrs and the general resurrection of the dead.

12

THE BOOKS OF ENOCH

The period of apocalyptic literature spanned from roughly the second century before Christ to the end of the first century of Christianity, from 200 BC to AD 100. While there is one major apocalyptic book in each Testament of the Bible—Daniel in the Old Testament and Revelation in the New Testament—a great deal of nonbiblical writings were also produced during that period. These works are widely referred to as "para-biblical," "intertestamental," or, more commonly, the "pseudepigrapha." By the end of the nineteenth century an effort was made to compile and edit these works. The most recent is a two-volume work edited by James H. Charlesworth on the pseudepigrapha (1983, 1985). The first volume of this collection is subtitled *Apocalyptic Literature and Testaments*. The second volume is subtitled *Expansions of the "Old Testament" and Legends, Wisdom and Philosophical Literature, Prayers, Psalms and Odes, Fragments of Lost Judeo-Hellenistic Works*.

The writings compiled by Charlesworth date from the second century BC to the ninth century AD. He gives examples, particularly in the first volume, of how apocalyptic literature made use of important figures from Jewish history and folklore. Among these works are the Syriac and Greek Apocalypses of Baruch (2 and 3 Baruch), the Apocalypses of Elijah, Adam, Abraham, Daniel, and Zephaniah, the Testament of Job, and four books attributed to Ezra.

Enoch

The character of Enoch is a sixth-generation descendant of Adam, and he is briefly featured in Genesis 5:19, 21–24. Immediately following the story of Cain and Abel (Gen 4), the fifth chapter of Genesis summarizes the generations between Adam and Noah. With each generation the Book of Genesis is rather methodical in its brief presentation of the life, age, and principal heir of that particular descendant of Adam. For example:

When Seth had lived one hundred five years, he became the father of Enosh. Seth lived after the birth of Enosh eight hundred seven years, and had other sons and

13

daughters. Thus all the days of Seth were nine hundred twelve years; and he died. (Gen 5:6–8)

With each generation, the depiction ends with the total life span of the descendant, concluding with the phrase "then he died" (Gen 5:5, 8, 11, 14, 17, 20, 27, 31).

With Enoch, however, the brief account ends differently. Whereas the other generations end with "then he died," Genesis says of Enoch, "Enoch walked with God; then he was no more, because God took him" (Gen 5:24). Herein lies a suggestion that Enoch did not die, but was taken directly to God while still living—like Elijah in 2 Kings 2:11.

This legend is expressed in a vast tradition of writings that developed from roughly 300 BC to AD 300. These writings celebrate and expand upon Enoch's ascent into heaven and give an account of his experiences there. Three principal writings are included in the collection by Charlesworth and are known simply as the three books of Enoch—the Ethiopic Apocalypse, the Slavonic Apocalypse, and the Hebrew Apocalypse of Enoch—or simply, 1 Enoch, 2 Enoch, and 3 Enoch.

The second book, or **Slavonic Apocalypse**, of Enoch—also known as the Book of the Secrets of Enoch—is an extended rendition of Genesis 5:21–32 that builds upon the events from Enoch to the flood. Enoch ascends to the seventh level of heaven, where he takes on angelic qualities. During this journey he sees both heaven and hell and eventually returns to earth, where he gives instruction to his children and others about what he had seen and learned in the heavenly realm. His experience provides an apocalyptic forecasting of humanity after death, for good and for bad. The book retains a strong monotheism while it also makes abundant use of mythology. The consistent theology is that God is the sole Creator.

The third book of Enoch, also known as the **Hebrew Apocalypse,** is dated from the third to as late as the tenth century AD, although Charlesworth dates it from the fifth to sixth centuries AD. It focuses on the ascension into heaven of Ishmael, a Palestinian rabbi who tours the six heavenly palaces and sees the throne and chariot of God. He receives revelations from the archangel Metatron.

Divided into forty-eight chapters, 3 Enoch has four main sections. In the first part (chapters 1—2) Ishmael passes through the six heavenly palaces; each palace is found within the previous one. At the gate of the seventh palace he is challenged by the guardian angels. God sends Meṭaṭron to allow Ishmael to enter. God receives him and sets him with the angels in the recitation of the heavenly Sanctus.

In the second part (chapters 3—16) Meṭaṭron is revealed to be Enoch himself, who describes the experience of his own ascension and transformation. In the third part (chapters 17—40) Enoch describes the organization of the heavenly world and gives an account of the hierarchies of angels and of the heavenly angelic liturgy. In the final part (chapters 41—48) Ishmael is shown the structure of heaven and the cosmos, the curtain of human history, which hangs before the face of God and depicts all history from Adam until the coming of the Messiah.

1 Enoch

The Ethiopic Apocalypse of Enoch is the major apocalyptic work outside the Bible. It is a composite work representing various writers from different periods. While fragments remain of a Greek and Latin translation, the Ethiopic version, translated between AD 350 and 650 for use by the Ethiopian church, is the most complete.[8] It comprises 107 chapters within a collection of five books known as the Enochian Pentateuch:

1. Book of Watchers (chapters 1—36)
2. Similitudes (Parables) of Enoch (chapters 37—71)
3. Astronomical Book (chapters 72—82)—describes a tour of the heavens
4. Book of Dreams (chapters 83—90)
5. The Epistle of Enoch (chapters 91—107)—within which is "The Apocalypse of Weeks."

While Enochian material circulated among Jews until the second century AD, it eventually fell out of favor due to discredited revolutionary interpretations. The original text of 1 Enoch vanished; however, the Greek text came to have an influence on early Christian works (see Jude 14). The book was discussed by various theological fathers of the church. Some, like Tertullian, regarded it as Scripture (On the Apparel of Women, 3),[9] while others, like St. Jerome, did not (Lives of Illustrious Men, 3).[10] Fragments of 1 Enoch were among the Dead Sea Scrolls discovered in 1947.

The title of book 1 of the Ethiopic Apocalypse of Enoch, the Book of Watchers, refers to the fallen angels who have intercourse with women of earth. It is an extended depiction of Genesis 6:1–4 in which the "sons of heaven" intermingle with human women on earth and beget by them what are referred to as Nephilim. The brief account—four verses in length—serves as a prelude to the story of the great flood. However, book 1 of 1 Enoch gives more detail to this story as it is told through the eyes of Enoch after "God took him" (Gen 5:24). Enoch intervenes on behalf of the people of earth but to no avail.

Book 2 of 1 Enoch, the Similitudes, deals with oracles and prophecies regarding heavenly realities and the imminent judgment of the righteous and the wicked. It has been suggested that there is an ascending progression to the parables that divides book 2 into three parts.

1. **Parable 1** (chapters 38—44)—judgment; cosmic secrets
2. **Parable 2** (chapters 45—57)—judgment of/by the eternal Son of man
3. **Parable 3** (chapters 58—69)—judgment by the elect one; blessedness of the righteous

Book 3, the Astronomical Book, is considered the oldest surviving Enochian material; it dates from the third century AD and has roots in the second. It describes time by the reckoning of the sun as shown to Enoch by the angel Uriel. Chapters 72—74 give the astronomical regulations regarding the sun and the moon. Chapter 75 concerns other heavenly luminaries and the progression of the four seasons. The cosmic structure is further extended to the four winds, the mountains, and rivers. A final summary is given in chapter 79.

Finally (chapter 80), Uriel describes the last period prior to the judgment when, true to apocalyptic form, the cosmic order collapses into disarray. The seasons are cut short, the seeds delay in sprouting, the rain is withheld, and the sky stands still (earthly perspective). The cycle of the moon will be altered and it will shine more brightly; many of the stars will change their courses (heavenly perspective).

The book concludes with Enoch being returned to his home, where he will relate these cosmic regulations to his son and encourage him to follow a law of righteousness so as to prepare for the time of judgment.

Book 4, the Book of Dreams, consists of two dreams that concern the future history of Israel from Enoch's perspective. This is an example of how apocalyptic literature uses an important figure of the past to make projections into its future from that character's point in history.

The first dream concerns the great flood of Genesis 6—7. The reference to the abyss is a typical reference to the ocean in ancient cosmology (see Gen 1:2). Enoch sees trees, the land, and mountains all being hurled into the depths of the abyss. Upon waking, Enoch offers a prayer to God to spare both the righteous and the generation descended from Enoch during the flood.

The second dream concerns the history of Israel from Adam to the Maccabean revolt. True to the style of apocalyptic literature, it is presented with dynamic imagery that makes use of symbols to express the various stages and figures. In the beginning the rise of a bull and a cow symbolizes the rise of Adam and Eve. Their offspring, the dark and red calves, of which the red is gored by the dark, parallel the story of Cain and Abel. The falling of the stars parallels the sinfulness of humanity's co-mingling with heavenly beings, which leads to the great flood. The remaining chapters of book 4 follow a symbolic progression of the history of Israel in which the meaning of the images are understood as follows:

Oxen (cows)—patriarchs
Sheep—faithful Israel
Beasts/birds of prey—pagan/Gentile oppressors
Horned sheep—Jewish leader
White bull with great horns—Messiah

Within the symbolic imagery are parallels to Abraham, Isaac (and Ishmael), Jacob (and Esau), and his twelve sons (89:10–12), as well as the story of Joseph up to the Exodus (89:13–27). The imagery continues through to the conquest of Canaan, the judges and the building of the Temple, the schism and the Exile, up to the Maccabean revolt. Chapter 90, the final chapter of book 4, depicts history from the Maccabean dynasty to the messianic era.[11]

The first book of Enoch concludes with book 5, the Epistle of Enoch. It is a summary on the theme of righteousness and sinfulness, blessedness and sorrow. Sorrow is bestowed upon the sinful, who are associated with the wealthy and powerful who exploit and oppress.

Within book 5 is featured the Apocalypse of Weeks, which consists of 91:12–17 and 93:1–10. First, weeks 8 through 10 are described, then weeks 1 through 7. The Apocalypse of Weeks describes a progression of the rise of deceit and sinfulness up through the seventh week. It concludes with the rise of righteousness in week 7, the eventual judgment for the sinner, and vindication for the righteous in weeks 8 to 10, leading to an indefinite period of goodness and righteousness.

Agents of Good and Evil in 1 Enoch

The personification or chief agent of evil in 1 Enoch is true to the tradition of apocalyptic writing. As such, Satan makes an appearance in 1 Enoch; however, various angels fulfill Satan's will. First Enoch 54:6 speaks of people of the earth being led astray by the "messengers of Satan," which implies that Satan enjoys supremacy over the wicked angels.

Other angels also serve the role of adversary:

> And the fourth voice I heard expelling the demons and forbidding them from coming to the Lord of the Spirits in order to accuse those who swell upon the earth.
> (1 Enoch 40:7)[12]

Some of these demons are named. Semyaz leads the angels who fornicated with the women of earth prior to the deluge and thus begot the Nephilim (6:3). Azaz'el (in the tradition of the Greek Titan Prometheus) teaches men the art of weapon making, and teaches women the art of seduction by means of jewels and cosmetics (8:1). Gadr'el is credited with misleading Eve (69:6).

Countering the evil angels is a host of heavenly angels and archangels, some of whom are named. In the Book of Watchers (book 1) Michael, Gabriel, and Surafel observe the evil of Azaz'el and Semyaz and resolve to deal with them in the name of the Most High (1 Enoch 9). Raphael is commanded by God to bind Azaz'el and throw him into the darkness (10:4). Phanuel (54:6) is prominent in the Similitudes (book 2) and is powerful enough to be named only fourth to Michael, Raphael, and Gabriel. Finally, Uriel acts as guide to Enoch in the Astronomical Book (book 3).

STUDY QUESTIONS

What Do We Mean by "Apocalyptic" Literature?

1. What are some characteristics of apocalyptic literature?
2. At what times, and for what purpose, were the apocalyptic books of the Bible written?
3. How did the Hebrew mindset differ from that of other ancient Near Eastern cultures?
4. *When something is described as "apocalyptic," what images or emotions does that invoke?*
5. *Is there a recent or historical event you can think of that can be described as apocalyptic? Why so?*
6. *With what other words can an "apocalyptic" experience be described?*

Apocalyptic Eschatology

1. What is the difference between prophetic and apocalyptic eschatology?
2. What is the difference between the literal and the symbolic interpretations of the thousand-year reign (millennium)? What is the Catholic Church's attitude toward the literal interpretation?
3. Who is Enoch? Name some of the chief apocalyptic elements in 1 Enoch.
4. *How do you imagine the event of the second coming of Christ or the end of the world?*

19

2
APOCALYPTIC PROPHECY

Under the reigns of Kings David and Solomon (1010–931 BC) the tribes of Israel were united as one kingdom under one king. After the death of Solomon, the united monarchy was split between his two rival sons, Jeroboam and Rehoboam. This resulted in a schism in 922 BC and divided Israel into two kingdoms. The northern kingdom of Israel, with its eventual capital in Samaria, encompassed ten of the twelve tribes of Israel. The southern kingdom of Judah, which occupied Jerusalem and the Temple, consisted of the tribes of Judah and Benjamin.

While the monarchy of Judah remained consistently Davidic in its succession, the kingdom of Israel underwent a shift of over four dynasties. While two of them remained in power for nearly 140 years, the beginning and the end of Israel as a separate kingdom were marked by instability and coups, as various factions vied to obtain and maintain power. With this instability came religious corruption. Pagan worship flourished throughout the northern kingdom, giving rise to prophetic opposition to both the social and political establishments. It was in the northern kingdom of Israel that Elijah and Elisha flourished, bringing about the downfall of the dynasty of Omri and the rise of Jehu. The prophets Hosea and Amos (who was from the south) were also called to preach to the northern kingdom.

Finally, in 722 BC the northern kingdom fell to the forces of Assyria led by Tiglath-Pileser III. The conquest resulted in the dispersion of the tribes within it (the ten lost tribes of Israel), and left only the southern kingdom of Judah.

In contrast to the kingdom of Israel, the southern kingdom of Judah maintained one monarchical dynasty in its 450-year history. Whereas instability and coups plagued the kingdom in the north, the monarchy of the south was often troubled by assassination, deposition, or extortion by foreign rulers. However, the house of

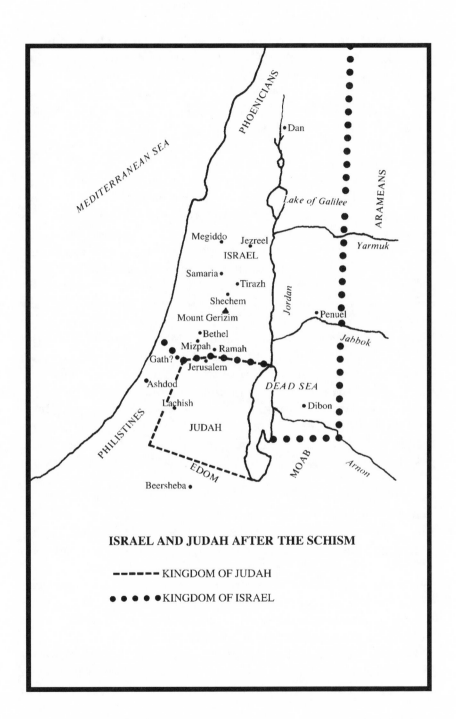

PHOENICIANS

MEDITERRANEAN SEA

• Dan

Lake of Galilee

ARAMEANS

Megiddo •   • Jezreel

ISRAEL

Yarmuk

Samaria •

• Tirazh

Jordan

Shechem

▲ Mount Gerizim

• Penuel

Jabbok

• Bethel

Mizpah • • Ramah

Gath? •

Jerusalem

DEAD SEA

• Ashdod

Lachish •

• Dibon

JUDAH

EDOM

MOAB

Arnon

PHILISTINES

Beersheba •

ISRAEL AND JUDAH AFTER THE SCHISM

------ KINGDOM OF JUDAH

● ● ● ● ● KINGDOM OF ISRAEL

David always managed to overcome such setbacks. This was interpreted as a manifestation of God's fidelity to the house of David, to whom was promised prosperity and protection (2 Sam 8—16).

In 587 BC, King Nebuchadnezzar conquered what was left of the southern kingdom of Judah. He destroyed the Temple and forced most of the people, but not all, into an exile that lasted forty-nine years. The remnant left in the region of Judah (known from thenceforth as "Jews") either remained in the region or, according to Jeremiah 41—45, fled to Egypt and disappeared into history. In 538 BC the kingdom of Babylon was conquered by the Persians. This event was followed by the Edict of Return under King Cyrus of Persia, which allowed the Jews to return to their homeland.

For the Jews who went into exile, an entire generation had lived all of their lives in Babylon. Having never seen Jerusalem nor experienced the cult and worship of Yahweh, a majority of Jews did not return to Jerusalem and to the land once promised to their ancestors. The remnant that did return rebuilt the Temple and lived as a Temple community within the Persian Empire. They did not, however, reestablish the Davidic dynasty because Persia remained the dominant empire of the region. The Temple, therefore, became the economic and religious center of the people.

To help in this restoration, principal writings comprising both the Law and the Prophets were compiled into what developed into the Jewish Torah, which codified the writings and precepts of the Jewish faith. The Torah became the foundation of the Restoration (Neh 8:1–12).

The return to the Promised Land and the Restoration of the Temple and the cult of Judaism were not without conflicts. Inevitably tensions arose between the returning exiles and the current occupants of Jerusalem. Tensions also arose among those who had returned over how best to restore the faith and the kingdom. While the number of Jews returning from Babylon may have been small, there would have been tension between the peasant farmers who had stayed behind and the returning Jews, some of whom would have taken possession of land they had previously owned, or claimed to have owned before the Exile. Political conflict would have arisen between the proponents of the Jerusalem Restoration and those remnants of the northern kingdom who still resided in the regions of Samaria (hence the bitter association with Samaritans). In addition to this, as is told in Ezra 9:1–2 and Nehemiah 9:2 and 13:23, tensions and sanctions arose against foreigners, and particularly against Jews who had intermarried with people of foreign extraction and thus produced a generation of half-breeds, who were regarded as a desecration of the holy race.

Israelite Prophecy

The period of apocalyptic literature spanned roughly from the second century before Christ to the end of the first century of Christianity (200 BC–AD 100). Apocalyptic literature is rooted in the late prophetic period, out of which grew the writings of Malachi, Zechariah, Joel, and parts of Isaiah and Ezekiel. This early period is known as the proto-apocalyptic period. Different terms have been used in the development of apocalyptic literature; however, the flow of the literature at this point, while still of a prophetic genre and tradition, was developing in an apocalyptic direction.

Prior to the Babylonian Exile the prophets and the kings were closely connected. This was the case in both Judah and Israel. While the monarchies concerned themselves with politics and the preservation of their kingdoms, the prophets and the prophetic class were concerned with keeping both the sociopolitical and the religious life of the kingdoms faithful to the precepts of the Mosaic covenant, the foundation of Hebrew faith. Pre-exilic prophecy tended to focus on the foreign policy of Israel and was concerned with kings and nations. This was particularly true during the wars against Assyria and Babylon, when Israel and Judah sought foreign alliances to help in the fight against their enemies. The prophets encouraged the people and the leaders to "put not your trust in princes" but rather on the promises made by God to the people and (in the case of the south) the house and monarchy of David.

After the Exile, however, it was the priestly and scribal class, not the prophets, who reorganized Israel and reestablished Judaism. Prophetic activity focused on the eschatological. It looked beyond the present to a new day, a new age, and a new hope. With flaws arising in the manner of restoration, much prophetic expectation began to focus on a restoration of the covenant, the kingdom, and the rule of David brought about not by the people, but by God himself. Prophetic writings of this period frequently made statements that included the phrase "in days to come" or "on that day," thus referring to Yahweh's imminent victory.

As part of the development of these themes, in order to bring about the impact intended, prophetic writings began to make use of imagery and language that would eventually distinguish the apocalyptic style. We begin to see the storm imagery (or storm theophany) of the ancient Canaanite mythology of Baal applied to the presence and power of Yahweh (see Fig. 2 on the next page). As Yahweh is beyond the human, his

The god Baal shown as god of the storm with the lightning spear and thunder club.

intervention would be expected to have a much grander, more awesome, and more catastrophic impact than mere human efforts. Hence, God's intervention for restoration would include such images as the collapse of the cosmos; the swift defeat, judgment, and eradication of the enemies of Israel and the covenant; and the establishment of a new kingdom, the restoration of the Davidic dynasty as a continuation of his promise encompassed in a new covenant. As God would be intervening to bring about all this himself, the expectation was that the Restoration would last forever.

Since apocalyptic literature is rooted in the late prophetic period, some of the earliest examples of apocalyptic texts are found in the later biblical prophets. The major prophetic writings to come out of this period are Ezekiel and Isaiah 24—27 (the Apocalypse of Isaiah) and 56—66 (Third Isaiah). Other writings of this time include Haggai, Joel, Zechariah, Malachi, Jonah, Zephaniah, and 1 and 2 Chronicles. Such prophets as Haggai and Zechariah sought to give encouragement to the Jews who returned from the Exile and pushed for the rebuilding of the Temple. Malachi strongly advocated a purity of worship.

Figure 2

ANCIENT CANAANITE MYTHOLOGY

Rains provide life in the desert

Baal—god of rain (therefore god of harvest, life, and fertility)
(manifested in lightning/thunder/shaking of the earth)

Yam—god of the sea/abyss (therefore god of darkness and chaos)
(manifested in Leviathan/sea serpent Rahab)

Mot—god of desert (therefore god of death)

Baal ——— fights ——→ **Yam** ——— is devoured by——→ **Mot**
(god of harvest)   storm battle   (god of sea/chaos)   (god of desert/death)

- The storm comes over the sea, who fights to keep it back—Yam fights Baal
- The storm comes ashore and provides the rain—Baal is declared king
- Banquet is declared—spring harvest
- The storm is swallowed by the desert as it moves farther eastward—Mot swallows Baal
(Cycle repeats itself in a cyclical view of the cosmos)
See also 1 Kings 17—18; Elijah preaches against the cult of Baal

Yahweh replaces Canaanite gods after occupation of the Promised Land

Yahweh ——— fights ——→ **Chaos** ——— devours ——→ **Death**
    storm theophany

- Yahweh rides in on the clouds (see Pss 18 and 29)
- Conquers the sea, bringing order to chaos
- Banquet is declared celebrating victory over enemies—see Isa 25:6–9
- Yahweh, unlike Baal, swallows death—is not swallowed by death
(Early apocalyptic prophecy portrays God's ultimate victory over death; no cyclical pattern—see Isa 25:8)

Zephaniah

Some prophets from earlier periods were developed, edited, and reinterpreted for a later period. Zephaniah is one such prophet who wrote during the period of the Assyrian war against Judah (640–622 BC). Zephaniah speaks of the final destruction of Baal by God (he focuses on Baal, not on Canaanite religion). In apocalyptic imagery he describes the "host of heaven" as the cosmic images of sun, moon, and stars—the images of the cosmic order, worshiped by Assyrians on their flat rooftops (Zeph 1:5). He further speaks of the "Day of the Lord" (Zeph 1:8) and the "Day of Wrath" combined with the image of storm theophany to describe God's coming down to conquer the chaos of pagan worship (Zeph 1:15–16). It is from these passages that the funeral chant "Dies irae, dies illa" is drawn, which is the first line of the sequence that used to be chanted or recited during the traditional Latin requiem Mass.

Haggai

It is generally assumed that Haggai was a Judean who had returned from exile, but no evidence confirms this. He speaks eloquently in favor of rebuilding the Temple, despite excuses about economic and financial woes. The Temple's importance was not so much as a place of worship, however, but rather as the place of Yahweh's presence. This may indicate that Haggai was a cultic prophet, while his emphasis on the importance of the king, Zerubbabel, may suggest he was a court prophet.

Haggai begins by speaking of the economic woes as possible reasons for the delay in rebuilding the Temple (Hag 1:5–6, 9–11). In response, God stirs up Zerubbabel to begin work (Hag 1:14), promising that the future glory of the new Temple will surpass that of the old. Haggai expresses the conviction that God will bring about prosperity once the people bring about the Temple (Hag 2:15–19). On an apocalyptic note, these promises include a glorious future that is introduced by God's shaking of heaven and earth (Hag 2:7, 21).

Zechariah

Writing around 520 BC, the prophet Zechariah pushes for the Temple to be completed in Jerusalem. In order to push for its reconstruction he agrees with Haggai's assertion that the Temple is the dwelling place of God. The book is divided into two parts (chapters 1—8 and 9—14)—some scholars believe three (chapters 1—9, 9—11, and 12—14)—all of which share a view of Jerusalem at the center of the world's destiny and a universal view of other nations looking to Jerusalem. This is an image that goes beyond the political borders of Israel itself.

The first part of Zechariah, chapters 1—8, incorporates eight symbolic visions that emphasize the rebuilding of the Temple. These images are used in later writings that are of a more pure apocalyptic (as distinct from prophetic) style. All of these images are made in relation to the Israel of Zechariah's time. They show a greater sense of the importance of God's action, but a reduced sense of the people's initiative.

1. **The Four Horsemen**	1:7–17	Relative peace for the world
2. **The Four Horns** and **Four Blacksmiths**	2:1–2	Nations that put down Judah, Israel, and Jerusalem
	2:1–4	The ones who will put down the horns
3. **The Surveyor**	2:5–17	The Restoration of Jerusalem
4. **Joshua the High Priest**	3:1–10	The purification of the priesthood
5. **The Lampstand** and the **Olive Trees**	4:1–3	The eyes of God, mastering the earth
	4:11–14	The anointed ones of Israel (kings/priests?)
6. **The Flying Scroll**	5:1–4	A curse on the world for theft and perjury
7. **The Woman in the Bushel**	5:5–11	The removal of guilt from Judah
8. **The Four Chariots**	6:1–8	Unrest on earth enables the rise of Judah

The second part of Zechariah, chapters 9—14 (often divided into two parts—see above), is more of an apocalyptic genre than the first. Accredited to another author who incorporated it into Zechariah's initial prophecy (chapters 1—8), Zechariah 9—14 consists of a messianic vision of the coming of the Prince of Peace. The image of the triumphant yet humble appearance described in Zechariah 9:9 is taken up by all four evangelists in their description of Jesus' entry into Jerusalem. Matthew quotes Zechariah 9:9 (and Isa 62:11) directly in his description of the event. Zechariah ends with an apocalyptic vision of a future time in which conflict will end in victory for God's faithful. The Messiah will bring universal peace and be acknowledged as the leader of the world.

Malachi

Scholars believe that the Book of Malachi was written around 455 BC. It advocates purity in the worship of the restored Temple. Malachi includes dynamic imagery that hints at an imminent judgment for impure practices. In this context, the third chapter begins with the coming of a messenger:

> See, I am sending my messenger
>   to prepare the way before me;
> and the LORD whom you seek
>   will suddenly come to his temple.
> The messenger of the covenant in whom you delight—
> indeed, he is coming, says the LORD of hosts.

In Matthew 11:10 Christ quotes this passage in reference to John the Baptist, and, in the early chapters of the Gospel, Matthew hints at it in regard to the Baptist's ministry. In the case of Malachi, the reference is to a messenger who will also bring about judgment and purification (Mal 3:3–5).

Malachi concludes with the final words of the Old Testament, in which the people are called to remember their tradition in the Mosaic Law and in God's continued communication with them in and through the prophets. The people are called to prepare the way for the Day of the Lord: a day spoken of as being both "great" and "terrible," but also one of a renewed conversion to the covenant (Mal 4:4–5). They prepare for the Day of the Lord by a renewal in the two principal aspects of Jewish scriptural tradition: the Law and the Prophets—in remembering (and returning to) the Law, and in the expectation of Elijah's return to fulfill a role of reconciliation.

> Remember the teaching of my servant Moses,
>   the statutes and ordinances
>   that I commanded him at Horeb for all Israel.
> Lo, I will send you the prophet Elijah
> before the great and terrible day of the LORD comes.
> He will turn the hearts of parents to their children
> and the hearts of children to their parents.

These final verses of Malachi could be seen in a similar context to the Gospel accounts of the transfiguration, when Jesus is seen in the presence of Moses, the father of the Law, and Elijah, the father and prototype of the prophets (Matt 17:1–13; Mark 9:2–13; Luke 9:28–36). In Matthew and Mark, a discussion regarding Elijah's return follows the transfiguration.

In the context of Malachi, however, the Day of the Lord refers to the renewal of the covenant and the Restoration of Temple worship. However, further development of prophetic literature will yield examples of a growing apocalyptic trend that goes beyond the present hopes and expectations of Israel.

While Zephaniah, Haggai, Zechariah, and Malachi contain some apocalyptic imagery, their writings are still in the nature and style of the traditional prophetic literature of Israel. It is from this period, however, that writings began to exhibit more apocalyptic qualities. These writings, rooted in the prophetic tradition, began to look beyond the prophetic expectation of the restoration of a worldly kingdom of Israel, and to a new day, a new age, and a new hope. While not yet incorporating a heavenly mediator to a human recipient within a narrative framework, symbols and imagery begin to emerge that will have a strong presence in later apocalyptic writing.

Among the apocalyptic prophets found in the Scriptures are Isaiah 24—27, and Ezekiel 38—39.

Isaiah 24—27—The Apocalypse of Isaiah

The Apocalypse of Isaiah speaks of cosmic judgment and a victory over death, incorporating signs and host figures from the heavens. It is not a narrative, however, and does not incorporate weird or bizarre symbolism. There is no heavenly intermediary, nor is there any calculation of history, time, or the seasons. However, images reflecting the Canaanite figures of Mot and Yam are present in Isaiah 27:1ff. Among the enemies named in Isaiah's apocalypse is Moab, which is set up as a general symbol for all of the enemies of Yahweh.

Chapter 24 begins the Apocalypse of Isaiah with a cosmic collapse (v. 1), a laying waste of the land that affects everyone of every class

(v. 2). Verse 4 states that "the heavens languish together with the earth," indicating that this collapse will affect all of creation. Verses 7–9 declare the party of feasting and wine-drinking to be over. The merriment has been turned into groaning. In place of the revelry, rebellion will weigh down the earth (v. 20). In the end, Yahweh will vanquish the rebellion throughout creation, and will reign as king (v. 23).

The "ancient covenant" referred to in verse 5 most likely means the covenant with Noah made after the flood (Gen 9:11–16), a covenant made with creation and with "all mortal creatures on the earth." The opening of the "windows on high" (Isa 24:18) recalls the "floodgates" of the deluge (Gen 7:11b). The action implies that God's "ancient covenant" with Noah against destroying the world in this way is null and void because of the people's sinfulness. Violating the "ancient covenant" is, therefore, a violation of the natural law, resulting in the pollution of the earth (v. 5). In turn, the earth and the cosmos—the natural world whose laws have been violated—collapse because of human sin (v. 6).

The Apocalypse of Isaiah continues in chapter 25 with an image that reflects the Canaanite myth of Baal, presented in terms of the reign and victory banquet of Yahweh. The banquet celebrates a victory over death itself. Whereas Baal is swallowed by Mot, the desert god of death, Yahweh destroys—or swallows—death forever (25:8). Therefore, Isaiah asserts Yahweh's dominance over Baal because Yahweh celebrates a victory that Baal does not win.

As Christians we can see a foretaste of the Eucharist in both the victory over death and in the banquet for all people. Isaiah 25:6–9 is also a popular option among the readings for a funeral liturgy, because the passage speaks of God destroying the veil of death forever. In God's divine plan (v. 1) the king, Yahweh, is an aid to the poor (v. 4). A victory banquet is declared for *all* people—not just Israel—because the veil (death) that darkens all people will be torn down (vv. 7–8a).

Yahweh is the great vindicator in Isaiah 26, trampling down the arrogant and lifting up the humble (vv. 4–5)—a theme we will later hear in Mary's Magnificat (Luke 1:52). Here, the people do nothing but wait for the Lord to do the work and they take refuge against Yahweh's vindication (vv. 20–21). Isaiah 26:19 even speaks of a resurrection, which Christians see as fulfilled in Christ.

Just as Yahweh destroyed death (Mot) in Isaiah 25, so too in Isaiah 27 Yahweh destroys the great Leviathan:

> On that day the LORD
>> with his cruel and great and strong sword
> will punish Leviathan the fleeing serpent,
> Leviathan the twisting serpent,
>> and he will kill the dragon that is in the sea. (Isa 27:1)

After the victory, Yahweh will bring forth the harvest of which Israel will be a part (v. 12), for Yahweh will punish the nations, restore Israel, and bring the people back to worship in Jerusalem (v. 13).

Ezekiel 38—39—The Prophecy against Gog

The prophecy against Gog tells of a final attack against the newly restored Israel by its enemies, symbolized in Gog from Magog (the land of Gog). Magog is mentioned along with Gomer, Madai, Javan, Tiras, Meshech, and Tubal in the Book of Genesis. He is among the sons of Japheth and grandsons of Noah who are listed among the fathers of nations (Gen 10:2). Some scholars have proposed that Gog represents Cyrus of Persia or Alexander the Great. For the purposes of Ezekiel's prophecy, however, Gog is the prince of Meshech and Tubal, which are located around Asia Minor somewhere north of Palestine (Ezek 38:3).

Ezekiel's prophecy against Gog incorporates a series of "Thus says the Lord GOD" speeches in which are seen motifs of the divine warrior—the deity who marches at the head of an army and is usually depicted in images of a storm or a shaking of the earth. This was a standard divine warrior mark in ancient cultures, including the mythology of Canaan, in which the storm was a manifestation of Baal. Divine warrior images as applied to Yahweh are seen in Psalms 18 and 29. The stages of this divine march and battle in the prophecy of Ezekiel are laid out as follows:

The Preparation for Battle

1. **38:3–9**   God chooses Gog
2. **38:10–13** God plans the task

3. **38:14–16**   Gog versus Israel—"That the nations may know…"

The Battle

4. **38:17–23**   The earth shakes, the cosmos falls
5. **39:1–16**   Gog is destroyed; the battlefield is cleaned up
6. **39:17–24**   Victory banquet
7. **39:25–29**   Israel restored, spirit poured out, new creation ordered

Traditionally the enemies of Israel came from the north. With the rise of Greece and Rome enemies eventually began to attack from the west, but their assault would still have been on Israel's northern border unless it was from the sea. However, at the time of Ezekiel, Israel's enemies had attacked from the north. Even those enemies to the east, such as Babylon, attacked Israel via the north. They would not cross the desert directly, but would travel by way of the Fertile Crescent, which curved northwestward from the Tigris and Euphrates rivers and descended southward onto Israel.

In ancient Near Eastern mythology the mountain of the gods was also traditionally located in the north. In the prophecy of Ezekiel, Gog will lead a massive army against Israel from this abode of the gods. Gog, like Baal, will come with the suddenness of a storm and advance like a cloud (Ezek 38:9). Gog's army will be huge and Israel's small. However, God's power will be strong against great enemies, as is seen in his victory against the forces of Gog.[1] Baal/Yam imagery is also used to describe God's victory. God's manifestation involves a collapse of the cosmos and a shaking of the earth (Ezek 38:18–23).

God is in command of all that is happening. Rather than Gog taking the initiative to attack Israel, it is God who will draw the armies of Gog from the north—"I will turn you around and put hooks into your jaws, and I will lead you out with all your army" (Ezek 38:4). This expresses the reality that it is God who is leading Gog forth with his hordes to attack Israel. God will drag the monster with hooks in his mouth to attack the people.

Ezekiel prophesies that Gog's attack will be toward a people who live at "the center [navel] of the earth" (Ezek 38:12). In the biblical worldview, this would indicate the Temple on Mount Zion in Jerusalem, considered to be the place on earth where contact with the divine was the strongest. It was the umbilical cord between God and humanity, where life is present in its most concentrated form. Just as the umbilical cord at the navel of an unborn child is the point of greatest contact and nourishment between the child and its mother, so the navel of the earth, at the Temple, is where contact between humanity and divinity was at its greatest. In this image, the attack of Gog against those who live at the navel of the earth is also an attack against the divine, where its presence is the most manifest.

Ezekiel makes use of an honor-shame mentality that was common to the ancient Hebrews. In allowing the Hebrews to be overrun by the Babylonians and driven into exile, God, as well as the Hebrews, was shamed in the eyes of the pagans. To the surrounding empires Yahweh could not protect his people, his land, or his Temple. Now, in the Restoration of Israel, God restores his honor (see Fig. 3 below). God defeats Gog and restores Israel, that "all the nations may know" that God did not betray or abandon his people. Rather, God was punishing them for their infidelities. Now it is God who will raise them up again. God will restore his honor and the honor of his people. God will no longer be profaned. Thus "the nations may know me, when through you, O Gog, I display my holiness before their eyes" (Ezek 38:16).

Figure 3

RESTORATION IN EZEKIEL

Revival of Israel
Vision of the Dry Bones (37:1–14)
Vision of the Two Sticks (37:15–28)

Defeat of Israel's Enemies
Prophecies against Gog (38—39)

The New Temple (40—47)

In the third and final prophecy against Gog, it is God who brings about the final victory. All enemies will be buried and their weapons will be destroyed. After the victory, a feast will be declared to which all of creation will be invited. The excluded are now included in that not only humans, but animals as well—birds and beasts—will be invited to the feast (Ezek 39:17). These and other images of Old Testament apocalypse will be seen later, in the Book of Revelation.

STUDY QUESTIONS

1. How did prophetic activity change after the Babylonian Exile? To what did it look forward?
2. What is the "Day of the Lord" in the Book of Malachi? How does it apply to Jesus in the Gospels?
3. What elements in the Apocalypse of Isaiah appear in the Christian tradition?
4. What images from ancient Near Eastern mythology does Ezekiel appropriate for his prophecy against Gog?

3
THE BOOK OF DANIEL

BACKGROUND

Any discussion of apocalyptic literature must include the Book of Daniel. It is the principal apocalyptic work of the Old Testament. Much of the apocalyptic imagery found in the New Testament echoes the images found in this book. Modern scholarship generally agrees to the dating, historical setting, purpose, and genre of the book. Because of this, the Book of Daniel has been placed alongside the Books of Maccabees as coming from an intense period of conflict between the Jewish and Greek cultures following the death of Alexander the Great.[1]

While set in Babylon, the Book of Daniel was written during a time of Greek persecution of the Jewish faith (ca. 165 BC), the account of which is told in Maccabees. The experience sparked the Maccabean revolt and a rise in apocalyptic writings. Daniel is the major apocalyptic work to come out of that experience.

In seeking to interpret God's action and purpose in such an experience, the Book of Daniel effectively produces a theology of history. The tales and visions of Daniel present an inspired interpretation of the present situation and the historical development that led to the crisis so as to understand them in terms of God's actions, will, and purpose in the life and history of the Jews. The book sought to inspire the Jews to cope with their present crisis, maintaining their faith that the persecution they were suffering was only temporary and that God would eventually intervene to rescue them.[2]

In order, therefore, to understand Daniel's theology of history, one must look at the historical setting that sparked the crisis, the Maccabean revolt, and the writing of the Book of Daniel.

35

Historical Background

In 587 BC King Nebuchadnezzar conquered what was left of the southern kingdom of Judah, destroying the Temple and forcing most of the people into an exile that lasted forty-nine years. In 539 BC the Persians conquered the kingdom of Babylon. This event was followed by the Edict of Return under King Cyrus, which allowed the Jews to return to their homeland. As an entire generation of Jews had lived all of their lives in Babylon and had never seen Jerusalem, most did not return from exile.

Those who did return rebuilt Jerusalem and the Temple. The people lived as a Temple community within the Persian Empire for the next two hundred years. They did not reestablish the kingship of Israel since they were still under Persian domination. The Temple became the economic center of the people and the Torah became the foundation of the Restoration.

Throughout the Israelites' history, in their conflicts with Assyria, Babylon, and Persia, their principal enemies came from the east. With the rise of Alexander the Great, the enemies of Israel began to come from the west. Alexander and his forces from Greece conquered Persia in 333 BC, and with it, the territory around Palestine.

Alexander ushered in the Hellenistic age, which spread Greek thought and culture throughout his empire. He founded a number of cities, which he named Alexandria and which became centers of Greek culture. The Greek language came to replace Persian as the international language and replaced Aramaic as the principal language of the Palestinian region. With the fall of Persia, Aramaic itself splintered into different groups and dialects.

In 323 BC Alexander the Great died. His empire was eventually divided by four generals, from which grew four dynasties within the former Greek Empire. Biblical history is concerned with two of these dynasties: the Seleucid dynasty of Syria with its eventual capital at Antioch, and the Ptolemaic dynasty in Egypt with its capital at Alexandria.

In the initial division of Alexander's empire, Palestine fell under the control of the Ptolemies; under their rule it continued to enjoy political autonomy and religious liberty. It was during the

Ptolemies' reign over Palestine that Jews migrated to the cultural center of Alexandria, where they were exposed to Greek thought and culture. They began to translate the Hebrew Scriptures into Greek, and from this there emerged the "Septuagint" text, so named because of the tradition that seventy-two scholars (rounded down to seventy), working independently, are said to have developed exact translations of the Hebrew Scriptures into Greek. This also resulted in a rise of "Hellenistic Jews."

After 199 BC a battle ensued between the Ptolemaic and Seleucid empires in which the Seleucids under King Antiochus III conquered Palestine from the Ptolemies. His successor, Antiochus IV, began to assert more control over the culture of the empire in an effort to Hellenize the people, which now included the Jews of Palestine.

Antiochus IV believed himself to be the embodiment of Zeus and demanded to be worshiped as a god. He named himself Epiphanes—"the most high god of heaven"—and it is as Antiochus Epiphanes that he is known to history. In defiance the Jewish people referred to him as *epimanēs*—"lunatic."[3]

Antiochus Epiphanes allowed the office of high priest in Jerusalem to be obtained by corrupt means (2 Macc 4:7–20). He forbade the observance of Judaism, including Torah and circumcision, and thus attempted to bring about

Anitioches IV, "Epiphanes," attempted to Hellenize Judah. His brutal measures against the Jews led to the Maccabean War.

enculturation of the populace to the Greek way of life. Violation of this prohibition was punishable by death (1 Macc 1:41–50). This caused a split in loyalty within Israel between the Hellenistic Jews, who promoted the transformation of Jerusalem into a Greek city, and those Jews who saw such enculturation as an abomination.[4]

In 168 BC Antiochus took over the Temple of Jerusalem, setting up an altar to Zeus. The Jews highly objected and revolted under Judas Maccabeus in a guerrilla rebellion that drove out the Greeks. In 165 BC the Jews reoccupied Jerusalem and repurified the Temple. The event is celebrated to this day in the Jewish feast of Hanukkah.

After 165 BC Israel was ruled by king-priests descended from Judas Maccabeus. Under the Maccabean or Hasmonean dynasty Israel enjoyed relative independence. With the Roman conquest of 63 BC, however, the Maccabees were deposed and replaced by a Roman procurator.

Conflicts between Israelite and Hellenistic Cultures

With the occupation of Palestine by the Greeks, an inevitable conflict arose between the Hellenistic and Jewish cultures. This clash was further intensified by the Antiochene persecutions after the Seleucid Empire acquired the region from the Ptolemies. The clash between Jewish and Hellenistic cultures can be summed up in two arenas.

The first conflict occurred between the thought and culture of the two societies. As Hellenistic culture was dominant in the region there was an attraction of Greek *philosophia*. It maintained that wisdom comes from knowledge and the sciences. This was at odds with Jewish thought, which held that wisdom came from faith or "fear" of God. Hence, the conflict of thought and culture was between Greek philosophy of knowledge and Jewish wisdom based on faith.

The second conflict was the persecution that broke out under the reign of Antiochus Epiphanes. The persecution of Antiochus and his desecration of the Temple gave rise not only to the Maccabean revolt, but also to apocalyptic writing. The Book of Daniel is one such writing to come directly out of this experience in Jewish history.

Most scholars agree that Daniel was written around 168–165 BC, in the midst of the Antiochene persecution and the Maccabean revolt. While the book is set during the Babylonian Exile, the issues it addresses are directly related to the conflict and persecution the Jews experienced at the hands of Greek, not Babylonian, culture. The visions and tales of Daniel deal with conflicts between Hellenistic and Jewish societies. The principal points by which Daniel addresses these conflicts are:

1. God gives wisdom—wisdom does not come from knowledge and the sciences *(philosophia)*.

2. God saves from death—those under persecution should have faith in God's saving power.
3. Real power is with God, not the king.
   - God has power over history.
   - God brings down arrogant kings and gives power to God's holy ones.

While all three points are present in Daniel, points 2 and 3 are more dominant. Point 1 is more relevant in describing the principal characters and the blessings God bestows upon them as holy men or prophets.

Daniel

While the Book of Daniel received its title from the main character, Daniel himself is not a historical figure. Even though the book is set in a historical context (the Exile) and makes use of historical figures (such as Nebuchadnezzar and Belshazzar) it also contains many historical errors. Therefore it cannot be considered a historical book.

In biblical tradition, Daniel is referred to in different contexts as a traditional, archetypical figure of righteousness or holiness along with such figures as Noah and Job (see Ezek 14:14; 28:3). In Canaanite mythology, Dan'el was a figure who judged.[5] However, Daniel does not judge (except in the case of Suzannah). The name itself, Dan-i-el, means judge-my-god or "God is my judge," which indicates that judgment is not a part of Daniel's role. Rather he interprets the judgment of God (see Fig. 4 on the next page).

Daniel as a Unit

Daniel exists in two forms or canons. There are two ancient texts of the Old Testament: the Hebrew text (called the Massoretic) and the Greek text (called the Septuagint). The placement of Daniel within these texts varies.

In the Hebrew text the Book of Daniel is included among the last books of the Writings. As distinguished from the Law and the Prophets, the Writings include such books as Ezra, Nehemiah, Qoheleth (Ecclesiastes), and Lamentations, among others.[6] The

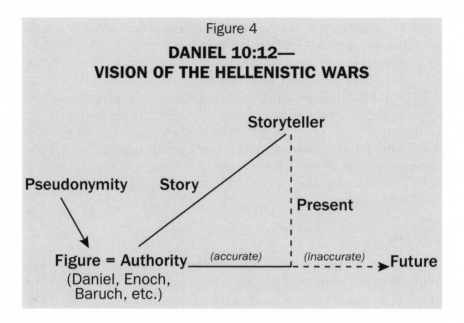

Figure 4

**DANIEL 10:12—
VISION OF THE HELLENISTIC WARS**

Hebrew text of Daniel consists only of chapters 1–12. It does not include chapters 13 and 14, the stories of Suzannah and the elders and of Bel and the dragon, nor the prayer of Azariah and the song of the three young men (3:26–90).

The Hebrew text is also written in two languages: Hebrew (Dan 1:1—2:4; 8:1—12:13) and Aramaic (Dan 2:4—7:28). In many Bibles you will note "[Aramaic]" inserted in 2:4, indicating where the Aramaic portion of Daniel begins. Why is this? No one knows for sure. (Aramaic was the language of the Persian Empire and came to replace Hebrew in Palestine. At the time of Christ, the regional language was Aramaic.)

In the Greek text, Daniel is located among the Major Prophets and follows the Book of Ezekiel. The Greek text of Daniel includes the stories of Suzannah and of Bel and the dragon in chapters 13 and 14, just as the prayer of Azariah and the prayer of the three men are included as additions to the story of the fiery furnace. While Catholic Bibles include these additions of the Greek text, this and other studies of Daniel focus only on chapters 1—12.

The Book of Daniel also contains two literary forms. The court tales (chapters 1—6) are told as third-person narratives set in the court of the king. While set within a particular period in Jewish history, the court tales deal with the issues encountered by the Jews under King Antiochus Epiphanes. Daniel and his companions seek to live and function within Babylonian society while remaining faithful to Jewish tradition. The tales consist of both test stories and vision stories. The tests are stories in which Daniel and his companions are faced with a choice of giving in to Babylonian culture or remaining true to Judaism. In the vision stories Daniel is called in to interpret a dream given to the king.

The second part of Daniel (chapters 7—12) consists of visions. These first-person narratives—"I, Daniel"—involve visions and angelic interpretation. Hence they are more apocalyptic in nature. It is in these passages that the book's theology of history is most eloquently spelled out. While they are set in Babylon during the Exile, they look toward the reign and persecution of Antiochus Epiphanes. They are meant to be portrayed as visions of the future (insofar as its setting) to offer meaning and hope for the present (insofar as its composition).

Daniel 7—12 interprets the history of the Hellenistic period up to the time of Antiochus. The four visions narrated are merely four different forms of the same vision. Each vision offers more compelling detail in its description and interpretation, leading up to the vision of Daniel 10—12, a thinly veiled history of the Hellenistic period (refer again to Fig. 4, the previous page).

Having presented a history of Israel up to the author's point in time, Daniel 11:40–45 then appears to foretell Antiochus's fate at the hands of God's direct intervention, told either as a specific prediction or as a curse. While Daniel 10:1—11:39 contains a degree of historical authenticity (because the writer was already aware of history up to his present time), Daniel 11:40–45 is a vision that did not historically come true. This is an example of how the narrative framework of apocalyptic literature mentioned in chapter 1 is applied to Daniel. The author sets his story in the past, catches up to the present, and projects Antiochus's fate into the future.

Finally, there are two settings of Daniel. The first is the historical setting inside the story itself, namely, the Babylonian Exile, which lasted from the fall of Jerusalem in 587 BC to the Edict of Return in 539 BC. However, the setting outside the story—the setting of the book's composition—is during the time of Antiochus Epiphanes. In order to understand the message inside the context of the stories, one must understand the context outside that prompted the writing of the stories themselves. While set within exile, the court tales of Daniel address the conflict that existed with the Hellenistic culture and persecution under Antiochus. Daniel's visions look ahead to the rule of Antiochus. They recount in symbolic language the history of Israel from the Exile up to the period of Antiochus's reign. (See Fig. 5 for a schematic diagram of Dan 1—12.)

Figure 5

OUTLINE OF DANIEL 1—12

	Chapter	King	Story type	
COURT TALES	1. Unclean food	Nebuchadnezzar	TEST	— Hebrew
	2. Dream	Nebuchadnezzar	VISION	Aramaic
	3. Furnace	Nebuchadnezzar	TEST	
	4. Tree	Nebuchadnezzar	VISION	
	5. Writing on wall	Belshazzar	VISION	
	6. Lions' den	Darius—Mede Cyrus—Persian	TEST	
VISIONS	7. Four beasts	Belshazzar		
	8. Ram/he-goat	Belshazzar		Hebrew
	9. Gabriel/ seventy weeks	Darius		
	10—12. Hellenistic wars	Cyrus		

THE MESSAGE OF DANIEL

When read and evaluated in terms of the Jewish experience of the Hellenistic period, each chapter of the Book of Daniel addresses the issues of both the conflict between Greek and Jewish cultures and the persecution under Antiochus Epiphanes. The court tales of

Daniel 1—6 deal with the three principal points mentioned in the introduction—that God gives wisdom, saves from death, and holds all kingly power. The apocalyptic visions of Daniel 7—12 address the history of Israel from the Exile to the present crisis with Antiochus.

A pattern can be seen in the Aramaic chapters of Daniel (chapters 2—7), in which the issues of power and delivery from death are addressed in a systematic way within the literary set-up of the book (see Fig. 6). The Aramaic chapters begin and end with stories that point to power being with God, specifically in the context of the four kingdoms following the Exile. A test against idolatry in which God delivers the faithful from death is told in the second and second-to-last chapters (chapters 3 and 6) of the Aramaic grouping. Finally, the two middle chapters deal with the issue of

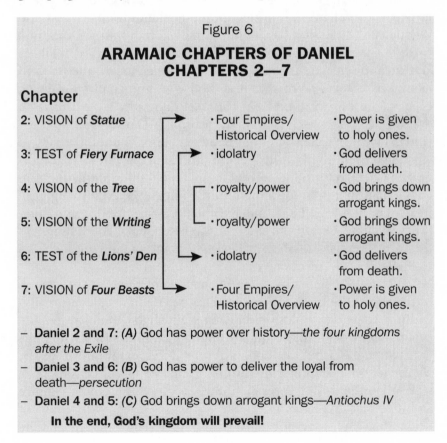

Figure 6

ARAMAIC CHAPTERS OF DANIEL
CHAPTERS 2—7

Chapter

2: VISION of *Statue* — · Four Empires/ Historical Overview · Power is given to holy ones.

3: TEST of *Fiery Furnace* — · idolatry · God delivers from death.

4: VISION of the *Tree* — · royalty/power · God brings down arrogant kings.

5: VISION of the *Writing* — · royalty/power · God brings down arrogant kings.

6: TEST of the *Lions' Den* — · idolatry · God delivers from death.

7: VISION of *Four Beasts* — · Four Empires/ Historical Overview · Power is given to holy ones.

— **Daniel 2 and 7:** *(A)* God has power over history—*the four kingdoms after the Exile*

— **Daniel 3 and 6:** *(B)* God has power to deliver the loyal from death—*persecution*

— **Daniel 4 and 5:** *(C)* God brings down arrogant kings—*Antiochus IV*

In the end, God's kingdom will prevail!

royalty, power, and arrogant kings. The themes are set up in the chapters in a sequence of A, B, C, C, B, A.

Daniel 1—6—The Court Tales

Daniel 1 begins with the story of young Daniel and his companions—Hananiah (given the Babylonian name Shadrach), Mishael (Meshach), and Azariah (Abednego)—being brought to the king's court to begin their enculturation into Babylonian (Chaldean) culture. Despite efforts at enculturation, Daniel and his companions do not eat the king's food, which they consider unclean for Jewish consumption.

The chapter begins by stating that it was God who gave Israel over to Babylon (v. 2). It goes on to describe how God had shown favor to Daniel by giving him the understanding of dreams and visions (v. 17). At the same time, verse 17 states—after the food episode—that God had given the four men a proficiency in all literature and science. As these were truly Greek ideals, the Book of Daniel makes the point that it is God who grants all knowledge, even in the case of Greek *philosophia*. Philosophy in and of itself does not bring about wisdom. Even though Daniel and his companions were in exile and under Babylonian domination it was God who gave them the knowledge and proficiency of their enculturation as a reward for being faithful to Jewish observance where eating Babylonian food was concerned. In the same way, even though the Jews were persecuted and under Hellenistic rule, God would grant them wisdom—and proficiency in Greek thought and culture—if they remained faithful to their Jewish heritage and did not succumb to Hellenistic persecution.

Daniel 2 begins the Aramaic chapters of the Book of Daniel. In the tale of the king's vision of the statue, Daniel presents a vision within a court tale. In his vision King Nebuchadnezzar foresees the development of history after his reign. The four successive kingdoms after the Babylonian reign of Nebuchadnezzar (gold) are the Medes (silver), the Persians (bronze), and the Greeks (iron). The feet of iron and tile represent the breakup of the Greek Empire and its being divided among four generals following the death of Alexander. The stone not hewn with human hands, which shatters the statue, is interpreted by Daniel to be a kingdom set up by God that will shatter the kingdoms and extend throughout the world. To the people of the time Daniel was written (ca. 168 BC) it was more likely intended to convey the faith and hope that God will deliver them from the oppression of earthly kingdoms and restore Israel under his dominion. As Christians, however, we can see a messianic implication to Daniel's interpretation.

The chapter reinforces key points regarding God. God is a God of heaven (vv. 18, 19, 28, 37, 44, 45). Wisdom and power belong to God (v. 20). God gives wisdom to the wise (v. 21). God reveals what is hidden (vv. 21, 22) and has revealed it to the king (vv. 28, 45). God is a God of gods and Lord of kings (v. 47), who makes and unmakes kings (v. 21) and has given dominion to Nebuchadnezzar (vv. 37–38). Finally, Daniel 2 assures the reader that God will set up a kingdom that will never be destroyed (v. 44).

Daniel 3 tells the dramatic, larger-than-life story of Shadrach, Meshach, and Abednego and their condemnation to the fiery furnace. Through this story, the Book of Daniel drives home the point that God will save from harm those who remain faithful and do not succumb to idolatry. Verse 15 challenges this up front with Nebuchadnezzar's question, "Who is the god that will deliver you out of my hands?" Verses 17–18 serve as an answer in which the three men assure Nebuchadnezzar that their God, whom they serve, can save them. However, even the Book of Daniel makes allowances for God's freedom when Shadrach, Meshach, and Abednego add: "Let him deliver us. But if not, be it known to you, O king, that we will not serve your gods and we will not worship [the idol] that you have set up." In the end, God sends the angel of deliverance to protect the men from the flames of the furnace (vv. 95–96). Here, as in the previous story, Nebuchadnezzar comes to declare the dominion of Israel's God.

The story of a second vision of Nebuchadnezzar begins in Daniel 3:98, but carries on through **Daniel 4.** The story of the king's vision of the tree and his subsequent madness is an adaptation of the tradition of Nabonidus, the last king of Babylon, who spent a number of years living in the city of Tema in Arabia, away from Babylon, and was resented by the Babylonian priests for his absence from temple responsibilities. Rumor claimed that he was mad or suffering from some sort of disorder. In a form of confession that was found among the Dead Sea Scrolls of Qumran, Nabonidus declares his sins before God, claiming that he had been afflicted with a form of inflammation for a number of years.[7] The author of Daniel changed the character of the story to the more historically prominent Nebuchadnezzar, but developed the story independently of the historical data regarding Nabonidus.

Where the message of the Book of Daniel is concerned, it is God who rules over the kingdoms of earth (vv. 22, 29, 31) and can give power to whomever he chooses (v. 14). God passes sentence (vv. 21–22) and for a time takes power and sanity away from Nebuchadnezzar, but eventually the king is restored. As in chapter 2, it is Daniel, with the spirit of God within him (v. 6), who interprets the king's dream, revealing God's judgment.

Unlike chapter 4, **Daniel 5**—the tale of the writing on the wall—deals with God's judgment against a king whose power is taken from him permanently. During a banquet given by King Belshazzar the sacred vessels of the Jerusalem Temple are used, expressing the disregard of Gentile kings for things considered sacred by the Jews. A hand appears, writing the words *Mene, Tekel,* and *Peres* on the wall of the banquet hall. Again, Daniel is summoned to interpret the message when the seers of the king's court fail to do so. That night Persian forces kill Belshazzar in their conquest of Babylon.

According to the Book of Daniel, Darius the Mede succeeds Belshazzar. Historically, however, while the first of three Persian kings named Darius eventually succeeded the throne in 522 BC there is no record of a "Darius the Mede." Further, it was Cyrus the Great of Persia who conquered the Neo-Babylonian kingdom of Chaldea. It was Darius I who later recaptured Babylon after it fell into the hands of a rebel.[8]

In this chapter it is stated yet again that Daniel is a man who has the spirit of God within him (v. 11). Therefore God is the source of Daniel's understanding of the writing. In his interpretation Daniel reiterates that it was God who gave Nebuchadnezzar his kingdom (v. 18) and that God rules over human kingdoms (v. 21). God's power is extended in verse 23b, when Daniel declares that it is God who holds life and rules over the whole course of life. It was

God who sent the message (v. 24). God, who measures kingdoms (v. 26), has measured the kingdom of Belshazzar. As he gave the kingdom to Nebuchadnezzar, God will take the kingdom away from Belshazzar and give it to the Medes and the Persians.

An interesting side note to the story of Daniel 5 is the reference to the shaking of the king's "hip joints" (v. 6). The verse states the reaction of Belshazzar from head to toe: "Then the king's face turned pale, and his thoughts terrified him. His limbs gave way, and his knees knocked together." (In the ancient mindset, it was believed that thoughts resided in the heart.) However, other Hebrew understandings for "his limbs gave way," which indicate that a mighty king collapsed or fainted, have been suggested: "his hip joints shook" or "his bowels were loosened," giving a rather irreverently humorous description of just how frightened this impious king became at the vision on the wall.

Like chapter 2, **Daniel 6** speaks to the issue of God's deliverance of those who remain faithful and do not give in to idolatry. The story of Daniel in the lions' den is perhaps the most widely known story of the book and certainly among the most widely known of the Old Testament. In the story, corrupt supervisors seek to denounce Daniel by influencing a law that prohibits petition to either god or man other than the king for a period of thirty days. After the law is passed they set a trap to catch Daniel in the worship of God. In verse 6 the supervisors acknowledge that valid accusation of Daniel is only done by way of God's Law. In following God's Law, Daniel is caught violating the very law created to denounce him. As in the case of Shadrach, Meshach, and Abednego, God saves Daniel from death. God sends his angel to protect Daniel from the lions (v. 23), moving King Darius to decree that the God of Daniel is to be revered and feared (v. 27).

Daniel 6:27b–28 is a summary of the main points of the court tales in Daniel; it emphasizes that God is "the living God enduring forever" whose "dominion has no end" (v. 27b). It goes on to state that God "delivers and rescues" (v. 28a). These important points of the court tales speak directly to the experience of the Jews under persecution by Antiochus. While Antiochus's reign is limited, God's is without end. While Antiochus threatens with death, God will save from death those who remain faithful to him.

Daniel 7—12—The Visions

There are four separate apocalyptic visions—the **four beasts, the ram and the he-goat, Gabriel and the seventy weeks,** and the **Hellenistic wars.** All reflect and foretell the development of history from Babylon to Antiochus. In short, they are four different forms of the same vision. Hence, they appear to be repetitive even within the individual visions themselves. Their underlying point, however, is the same as in the court tales. They are placed within the context of the rise of Hellenism and present a theology of history that emphasizes God's dominance over history and God's ultimate plan for the Jewish people.

Daniel 7 is the last of the Aramaic chapters and mirrors the message of Daniel 2 in its vision of the statue. The vision of the four beasts deals with the rise and fall of the four kingdoms following the Babylonian Exile. While it looks ahead to the future (being set in Babylon), it also looks back to chapter 2 and gives greater precision to the interpretation of Nebuchadnezzar's vision.

The vision begins as Daniel is lying in bed, but the scene shifts to heaven in verses 9–14 as the triumph of heaven is described in images similar to that of Baal coming on the clouds. The fourth beast is condemned and destroyed. The other beasts are deposed in due time (v. 12). Finally, "one like a human being" or "one like a son of man" receives glory, dominion, and kingship (vv. 13b–14). In verses 15–18 Daniel is in need of a heavenly interpreter in order to understand the vision. An explanation is given to him in the final part of Daniel 7 that gives particular focus to the fourth beast (vv. 19–27). Finally, Daniel concludes with the command that he keep the vision to himself (v. 28).

The images in this vision are grotesque. The beasts are not only beasts of destruction but are described as having bizarre, unnatural qualities—lion with wings, bear with tusks, leopard with four heads. The fourth beast is not described like the others, nor is it described with any clarity except with regard to its iron teeth (which represents Greece) and ten horns (representing the ten Seleucid kings prior to Antiochus Epiphanes). Antiochus's prohibition, corruption, and persecution of Judaism are reflected in the little horn who shall arrogantly "speak words against the Most High, shall wear out the holy ones of the Most High, and shall attempt to change the sacred seasons and the law" (v. 25). The three horns that were torn out of the way to make room for it rest on the presumption that three of Antiochus's predecessors died violently so he could succeed to the throne.[9] The accuracy of that presumption is shaky.

The "one like a human being" gives a human contrast to the grotesque images of the four beasts. The traditional interpretation is that the image refers simply to one who is or looks like a human being. "Son of man" is not a title, as it is in the case of Jesus Christ. Just as the four beasts are figures of the pagan empires who dominated the region following the Exile, the human form represents the "holy ones of the Most High" who will come to receive the kingship when the beasts are destroyed.

Other interpretations take more seriously the mythic background of the passage. Strife on earth is also strife in the heavenly world. Therefore, the conflict between Antiochus Epiphanes and the Jewish people is mirrored in heaven in that every person has his or her own heavenly representative. The "holy ones" are seen as angelic beings on the side of Israel, and Michael (of chapter 10) is identified as the "one like a son of man" who fights as Israel's champion in heaven. This second interpretation will be prevalent in the Book of Revelation.

The vision of the ram and the he-goat in **Daniel 8** is unique in the Book of Daniel in that it gives no explicit information about God. However, it is implied that the heavenly hosts are from God and that only God's hand knocks down kingdoms. As in the vision of chapter 7, Daniel needs an interpreter. The interpreter comes in the form of the archangel Gabriel (v. 16), who commands Daniel not to disclose the vision (v. 26b).

The explanation for the ram and the he-goat in this chapter is more specific than that of the four beasts. The ram with two horns (v. 3) explicitly signifies the kings of the Medes and the Persians (v. 20). The he-goat from the west (v. 5)—a new direction for the enemies of Israel—represents the Greeks, and the great horn is its first king (v. 21), Alexander the Great. The interpretation becomes more obscure, however, as the writer approaches the period of Antiochus. Antiochus is not specifically named in the interpretation of the vision, nor are the Seleucid or Ptolemaic kingdoms. However,

Antiochus is strongly implied when yet another "little horn" (v. 9) is again explained to symbolize "a king of bold countenance…skilled in intrigue" (v. 23f.). He is described as replacing the daily sacrifice with sin, casting down the sanctuary, and boasting against the prince of hosts (vv. 11–12), a close parallel to Antiochus Epiphanes.

The cry of "how long" (v. 13) is a common one of Old Testament lamentation. In the psalms, for example, we find it in Psalm 13 ("How long, O LORD? Will you forget me forever?" v. 1) and Psalm 74 ("How long, O God, is the foe to scoff?" v. 10). In Daniel 8 this cry is answered in terms of morning and evening sacrifices. Presumably it is an insertion by the author of chapter 8, who was interested in calculating the length of the persecution: 2,300 evenings and mornings (or 1,150 days) are understood as 2,300 morning and evening sacrifices (a practice that had just been described as removed by the little horn). This is not, however, understood to be a calculation of exact time, but rather an indication that the persecution will continue for some time yet. Verse 26b reinforces this notion.

Daniel 9, Gabriel and the seventy weeks, is also different from the rest of the Book of Daniel because it is an interpretation of an older biblical text. In this vision Gabriel returns to explain to Daniel the meaning of Jeremiah's prediction of a seventy-year exile. Historically the Exile lasted forty-nine years, from 587 to 538 BC, not seventy years, as had been predicted by Jeremiah (Jer 25:11; 29:10).

The context in which this reinterpretation comes about is the experience of Daniel's author, who lived during the persecution of Antiochus in the second century BC. The Exile lasted less than seventy years, and the Jews had long since returned from Babylon. However, the kingdom of Israel had still not been restored. The Jews were still under occupation and suffering persecution. Why was this so?

Daniel first offers a prayer acknowledging the sinfulness of the people, asking God to spare Israel their punishment (vv. 3–19). In answer to his prayer, Gabriel offers a reinterpretation of Jeremiah in which the prediction of seventy years is understood as seventy *weeks* of years. Just as a week of days is seven days, so a week of years is seven years. Seventy weeks of years can therefore be calculated to 490 years. This sum of seventy weeks of years is broken down in verses 25–27 into increments of seven weeks (of years), sixty-two weeks (of years), and one week (of years). These divisions of 49, 434, and 7 years add up to 490 years until the end of transgression.

Four hundred ninety years is roughly, but not exactly, the time between the Exile and the persecution of Antiochus. The exact time between the beginning of the Babylonian Exile to the end of the Antiochean persecution is 422 years. Hence, the resolution of Daniel 9 is that even though the people have returned from Babylon, the Exile continues under Antiochus. When it is over, there will be freedom, purification, and order. With roughly sixty-eight years to go before the end of the 490-year period, there would logically be a sense in Daniel 9 that the people are closer to the end than to the beginning. In any case, the Exile decreed by God through the prophet Jeremiah is understood as still going on under the persecution of Antiochus.

Daniel 10, 11, and **12** contain the last of the apocalyptic visions and the final event in the Hebrew text of the Book of Daniel. This is the vision of the Hellenistic wars. It is the longest and most elaborate vision of the book, and the most thinly veiled of the four apocalyptic visions. It repeats some of the material contained in the other visions of Daniel and is concerned with the history of the major kingdoms between Cyrus's conquest of Babylon and the end of Antiochus's reign. The unnamed angel offers Daniel a brief, general overview of the history of the Persian Empire and Alexander the Great. However, it is more detailed in its account of the Seleucid kingdom.

Although written during the time of Antiochus Epiphanes, the vision within the story is set during the time of King Cyrus of Persia (v. 1). Daniel 11:5–45 describes the history of the Ptolemaic and Seleucid dynasties. The Ptolemies are from the south while the Seleucids are from the north. Still, the author remains vague as to the specific identities of the royal figures described in the vision and does not give any specific names.

The author catches up to his own period by Daniel 11:39. In the verses following, the author offers a prediction regarding the fate of Antiochus in a vision that is less historical and more eschatological in nature. Like Gog in the Book of Ezekiel, Antiochus is a king from the north who will attack Israel and eventually fall in an apocalyptic battle. While Antiochus did not historically die in this matter, his death in Daniel's vision coincides with the eschatological triumph of Michael in the heavenly battle (Dan 12:1f.). As the angelic protector over Israel, his triumph in heaven becomes mirrored in Israel's deliverance from persecution.

The underlying goal of the apocalyptic visions of Daniel 7—12 is to help the reader to understand what is happening in light of the persecution under Antiochus Epiphanes: a theology of history that expresses God's ultimate control. God gives power to whomever he pleases. God bestows justice and punishment. God delivers from death, brings down the arrogant king, and gives the kingdom to the holy ones. Therefore, one must continue to be faithful and not succumb to the idolatry of the Greek/Hellenistic culture.

STUDY QUESTIONS

Background

1. What do we mean by a "theology of history"? How does the Book of Daniel produce a theology of history?
2. What types of conflict existed between Jewish and Greek (Hellenistic) societies after Alexander's conquest?
3. What are the three principal points repeatedly made in the court tales of Daniel?

The Message of Daniel

1. Which stories from Daniel deal with the following issues?
   • God's primacy over kings
   • God's protection against persecutions
   • God's power over history
2. What is the principal subject of the visions in Daniel 7—12? How does this relate to the "theology of history" discussed above?
3. How does Daniel reinterpret Jeremiah's prophecy of a seventy-year exile?

4
APOCALYPTIC THEMES IN THE NEW TESTAMENT

JUDGMENT AND THE SECOND COMING OF CHRIST

In the Hebrew Scriptures apocalyptic writing focuses on the Restoration of the kingdom of Israel and the Davidic dynasty under the auspices of the Mosaic Law. In the New Testament the focus of apocalyptic writing shifts to the emergence of the kingdom of heaven ushered in by the coming of Christ. Such focus can and does stand on its own as a point of faith, or is often spoken of as a means of instilling hope in a community suffering persecution. Just as the Jews under Antiochus looked to God to restore their freedom and prosperity in a new kingdom, so did the Christians who suffered persecution in the early church look to the second coming of Christ to defeat their enemies and usher in the new kingdom of heaven.

The New Testament letters speak of this eschatological expectation, particularly in light of persecutions and trials. The promise and expectation of Christ's coming is invoked to encourage patience in trials and persistence in living the Christian life so that one will be found ready and acceptable when Jesus comes again.

The Letter of James encourages its readers:

Be patient, therefore, beloved, until the coming of the Lord. The farmer waits for the precious crop from the earth, being patient with it until it receives the early and the late rains. You also must be patient. Strengthen your hearts, for the coming of the Lord is near. (Jas 5:7–8)

First John also alludes to eschatological events:

And now, little children, abide in him, so that when he is revealed we may have confidence and not be put to shame before him at his coming. (1 John 2:28)

This encourages Christians to remain faithful so that they will be assured acceptance at the coming of Christ.

In 1 Peter, Christ's coming is used as a consolation in the midst of trials:

...even if now for a little while you have had to suffer various trials, so that the genuineness of your faith—being more precious than gold that, though perishable, is tested by fire—may be found to result in praise and glory and honor when Jesus Christ is revealed. (1 Pet 1:6–7)

and again:

Set all your hope on the grace that Jesus Christ will bring you when he is revealed. (1 Pet 1:13)

Second Peter speaks frequently of the second coming, referring to it in regard to the behavior of Christians, while incorporating the image of cosmic collapse.

But the day of the Lord will come like a thief, and then the heavens will pass away with a loud noise, and the elements will be dissolved with fire, and the earth and everything that is done on it will be disclosed. Since all these things are to be dissolved in this way, what sort of persons ought you to be...? (2 Pet 3:10–11)

Finally, the Letter of Jude makes use of apocalyptic imagery in dealing with the issue of false teachers. He intermingles references to the past with expectations for the future by bringing into play events and people of the Old Testament in reference to expectations of the end times. Jude also mentions Sodom and Gomorrah, Cain, Balaam and Korah, from Scripture. He even speaks of Enoch and the "Assumption of Moses," both found amid the pseud-epigrapha.

St. Paul

Without a doubt St. Paul is the principal theologian of the New Testament, although to truly illustrate the depth of his influence would require several more chapters. St. Paul is believed to have written up to seven epistles, is credited by tradition for six more (although scholarly opinion would argue pseudonymity, or the practice of attributing a writing to a well-known person), and is believed to have influenced the theology of at least one Gospel (Mark), which in turn had an impact on the development of two more (Matthew and Luke). Scholarly opinion has placed the dates of all epistles attributed to St. Paul (AD 41–63) prior to the date in which it is believed the earliest Gospel, Mark, was composed (AD 64–67).[1] Therefore St. Paul holds particular prominence among the writers of the New Testament and in the development of early Christian theology. Even today, much of our Christian teachings rest on the solid foundation of the writings of St. Paul.

St. Paul frequently incorporates judgment and salvation when speaking of Christ's imminent return. In 1 Corinthians 1:8, for example, St. Paul writes: "[God] will also strengthen you to the end, so that you may be blameless on the day of our Lord Jesus Christ." However, the Pauline letters that have the strongest focus on eschatological themes are the letters to the Thessalonians. In these letters, St. Paul describes the events of the end times in ways that reflect some apocalyptic thought and that have been a strong influence on the apocalyptic expectations of today.

The Letters to the Thessalonians

Thessalonica was a port city of Macedonia, founded around 315 BC by Cassander, who was one of the generals of Alexander the Great. In 146 BC it became the capital of the Roman province of Macedonia, where it supported the troops of Octavius during the battle of Philippi in 42 BC.

During the lifetime of St. Paul, Thessalonica was an important economic, commercial, and political center, with a harbor and a location on the Egnitian Way (the main Roman road across the Balkans). Thessalonica was a thriving commercial center; it attracted a broad-based population, a Jewish population large enough to support a synagogue, and a pagan population that included thriving pagan cults. Egyptian and Roman sanctuaries to such gods as Isis, Serapis, Osiris, and Anubis have been discovered. Emperor worship also flourished.

The Acts of the Apostles does not present a full or accurate historical description of St. Paul's visit to Thessalonica (Acts 17:1–9). St. Paul, Silvanus, and Timothy came to the city during St. Paul's third missionary journey (ca. AD 50). St. Paul preached at the Thessalonian synagogue shortly after his expulsion from Philippi. The success of his preaching resulted in his expulsion. He escaped to Athens (Acts 17:10–15) and eventually sent Timothy back to Thessalonica (1 Thess 2:17–3:3) while he moved on to Corinth. It was in Corinth that Timothy rejoined St. Paul, bringing news of his visit to Thessalonica. Timothy's visit is spoken of and dealt with in St. Paul's first letter, which is believed to have been written just months after his departure from Thessalonica.

First Thessalonians is the earliest written book in the New Testament. Traditionally it was dated around AD 41–43, although recent scholarship has suggested a date of AD 50–51. It is the oldest literary evidence of how the early Christians attached significance to Christ's death and resurrection. The allusion to God the Father, the Lord Jesus Christ, and the Holy Spirit in the first ten verses shows how quickly trinitarian ideas became standard in Christianity by the middle of the first century, just twenty years after Jesus' ascension.

As the oldest existing Christian document this letter is also valuable from a literary standpoint. Historical, social, and religious factors prevented the development of a specifically Christian literature during the early years, but did not stop the writing of letters. Some see 1 Thessalonians as a type of personal letter, written according to the norms of letter writing in the Hellenistic world of the early Christian era. Therefore, it must be read as such—as a letter, as a form of communication. Hence, as a letter, Thessalonians is not in and of itself an apocalyptic document. Yet it speaks of themes that have had an impact on Christian eschatological thinking.

The issues and images found in 1 Thessalonians express Christianity's faith and hope in Christ's death and resurrection and his second coming. However, because they are couched in apocalyptic and therefore symbolic language and terminology, they cannot be taken literally. Rather they must be understood within the overall context of St. Paul's concern and those of the early church.

Early Christians generally believed that the second coming would occur within their lifetime. St. Paul deals with the fear that those Christians who had died prior to the second coming were without hope.[2]

> We do not want you to be uninformed, brothers and sisters, about those who have died, so that you may not grieve as others do who have no hope. (1 Thess 4:13)

To address this concern, St. Paul speaks of Jesus, who "died and rose again."

> For since we believe that Jesus died and rose again, even so, through Jesus, God will bring with him those who have died. (1 Thess 4:14)

First Thessalonians 4:13—5:11 deals with the apocalyptic theme of parousia, giving an illustration of the Lord's second coming within the context of Christ's salvation for those who have already died—in fact, *beginning* with it:

> For the Lord himself, with a cry of command, with the archangel's call and with the sound of God's trumpet, will descend from heaven, and the dead in Christ will rise first. Then we who are alive, who are left, will be caught up in the clouds together with them to meet the Lord in the air; and so we will be with the Lord forever. (1 Thess 4:16–17)

He further addresses the expectation of the second coming being soon, or at a particular time:

> Concerning the times and the seasons, brothers and sisters, you do not need to have anything written to you. For you yourselves know very well that the day of the Lord will come like a thief in the night. (1 Thess 5:1–2)

St. Paul even describes the Day of the Lord in terms of images—symbolic comparisons of an event not yet experienced.

> When they say, "There is peace and security," then sudden destruction will come upon them, as labor pains come upon a pregnant woman, and there will be no escape! (1 Thess 5:3)

In the very brief **2 Thessalonians** the Day of the Lord is an important issue. Dated between AD 51 and 52 and the late first century, 2 Thessalonians attests to a process of theological development with regard to the finality of Christian life, the final judgment against the wicked, and the salvation of the faithful at the coming of Christ. Therefore, unlike the earlier 1 Thessalonians, 2 Thessalonians is presented from the standpoint of teaching rather than shared eager hope.

Second Thessalonians disapproves, however, of the enthusiasm regarding specific times and places, or the nearness of the parousia. Whereas in 1 Thessalonians St. Paul gives a slight hint at disapproval—"you do not need to have anything written to you. For you yourselves know very well that the day of the Lord will come like a thief in the night"—in 2 Thessalonians he expresses strong disapproval of those who would seek to predict the second coming. He encourages the Thessalonians not to follow such notions:

> As to the coming of our Lord Jesus Christ and our being gathered together to him, we beg you, brothers and sisters, not to be quickly shaken in mind or alarmed, either by spirit or by word or by letter, as though from us, to the effect that the day of the Lord is already here. Let no one deceive you in any way. (2 Thess 2:1–3)

He does, however, hint that the second coming will be preceded by a period of lawlessness spearheaded by one who will lead people astray:

> Then the lawless one will be revealed, whom the Lord Jesus will destroy with the breath of his mouth, annihilating him by the manifestation of his coming. (2 Thess 2:8)

St. Paul puts this all within the context of encouraging the people of Thessalonica to remain strong in faith and steadfast in bearing witness to Christ in the midst of trials and falsehoods. Herein lies the purpose for such apocalyptic imagery:

> So then, brothers and sisters, stand firm and hold fast to the traditions that you were taught by us, either by word of mouth or by our letter. (2 Thess 2:15)

While St. Paul makes use of such symbols and descriptions, his principal point is one of encouragement, not of predicting or describing future events. While the recipients of his letter are undergoing various experiences as people of faith, both good and bad, he writes to emphasize the predominance of Christ's salvation and the immanence of victory in order to encourage the people to hold firm.

This becomes a predominant focus in the apocalyptic imagery found in the Gospels themselves.

The Eschatological Discourse

Composed after all of the Pauline epistles were written, the four canonical Gospels use apocalyptic imagery to reflect the expectation of the early church regarding Christ's second coming. While references to judgment and salvation are found throughout the Gospels, the Eschatological Discourse is found in three of the four Gospels: Matthew (24:1—25:46), Mark (13:1–37), and Luke (21:5–36), also known as the Synoptic Gospels.

In all three Synoptic Gospels the Eschatological Discourse is placed after Jesus' triumphant entry into Jerusalem (Matt 21:1–10; Mark 11:1–11; Luke 19:28–40), but does not follow immediately upon this event. In the Gospels of Mark and Luke, the discourse is placed right after his observation of the poor widow's contribution (Mark 12:41–44; Luke 21:1–4). Matthew, on the other hand, begins the Eschatological Discourse after a harsh criticism of the scribes and Pharisees (Matt 23).[3] All three evangelists use questions regarding the Temple as the springboard to Jesus' teaching and begin with a diatribe regarding the calamities that are to precede the end times.

While many interpret these portions of the Gospels as a list of what will happen at the end of the world, one must read the eschatological imagery within the overall context of the discourse. The following is a list of the key teachings that are found in the Eschatological Discourse (those in italics are teachings or parables unique to a particular Gospel):

- **The Temple** (Matt 24:1–3; Mark 13:1–4; Luke 21:5–7)—fulfilled in AD 70?
- **Beginning of Calamities** (Matt 24:4–8; Mark 13:5–8; Luke 21:8–11)
- **Beginning of Persecutions** (Matt 24:9–14; Mark 13:9–13; Luke 21:12–19)—fulfilled in early persecutions?
- **Great Tribulation** (Matt 24:15–28; Mark 13:14–23; Luke 21:20–23)—fulfilled in Jewish uprising and Roman response?
  - **Devastation** (Matt 24:15–22; Mark 13:14–20; Luke 21:20–23)
  - *Destruction of Jerusalem* (Luke 21:24)
  - **False Prophets** (Matt 24:23–28; Mark 13:21–23)
  - **Coming of the Kingdom** (Matt 24:23; Mark 13:21; Luke 17:20–21)
- **Coming of the Son of Man** (Matt 24:29–31; Mark 13:24–27; Luke 21:25–28)
  - **The Fig Tree** (Matt 24:32–36; Mark 13:28–32; Luke 21:29–33)
- **Need for Watchfulness** (Matt 24:36–51; Mark 13:32–37; Luke 21:34–36)
  - *Parable of the Ten Virgins* (Matt 25:1–13)
  - *Parable of the Silver Pieces* (Matt 25:14–30)
  - *Last Judgment* (Matt 25:31–46)

The reader must keep in mind the historical setting of the Gospels. By the time they were written—after the AD 60s and as late as AD 90—the early church had already experienced persecution on at least the local level. Nero's empire-wide persecution had taken place in the mid-60s. By the time Luke and Matthew were composed (AD 80–90) the Temple in Jerusalem had been destroyed by Roman forces in AD 70 as a result of the Jewish rebellion.

Therefore, to the early reader of these Gospels, much of what Jesus had prophesied had already taken place. Many believed that the destruction of the Temple would usher in the end, and yet the end had not come. Therefore, the destruction of the Temple was not interpreted as the precursor to Christ's return, but as the catalyst for Christians to travel the world so as to prepare all humanity for Christ's return.[4]

As Christians we still look for the return of Christ in glory. Therefore, lingering questions still persist throughout Christianity. When will the end come? What signs will precede the parousia and the Second Coming of Christ? In the midst of the many verses addressing this issue, the one point Jesus makes in all three Gospels is simple and direct: Be on guard! Be watchful! Let no one mislead you!

Two particular passages featured within this teaching are seemingly contrasting statements regarding the question of when these events are to occur.

> Truly I tell you, this generation will not pass away until all these things have taken place. (Matt 24:34; Mark 13:30; Luke 21:32)

and

> But about that day and hour no one knows, neither the angels of heaven, nor the Son, but only the Father. (Matt 24:36; Mark 13:32; not found in Luke)

Both passages have been applied closely to the event of the parousia and the Second Coming. While the first appears to reflect the common notion of early Christianity that Christ was coming very soon, the second appears to contradict that notion, or at least to keep it shrouded in mystery.

While the Gospels are not of an apocalyptic genre, one can still understand the Eschatological Discourse in the same manner as the images and format found in the Book of Daniel. From the standpoint of the author, the calamities had already occurred and Jesus' prophecies regarding them are written in hindsight. Just as the author of Daniel placed both the visionary and his visions in the past, so too do the authors of the Gospels recollect the words of Jesus in light of what has already happened.

The authors of the Gospels understood the "calamity" portion of the discourse—persecutions, wars, insurrections, rebellion, and the destruction of Jerusalem and the Temple—as having been fulfilled within the generation following Christ's ascension. Hence, the prediction regarding the present generation would fit better alongside the beginning of calamities, which must come prior to the divine intervention that Jesus speaks of.

On the other hand, the teaching regarding the Second Coming has not yet been fulfilled, nor is its time of fulfillment known; hence the need for watchfulness. This is where the authors of the Gospels project into the future the hope of Christ's imminent return. Therefore, placed in the overall context of early Christian experience, the progression of the Eschatological Discourse can be understood as follows:

1. Calamities, persecutions, and destruction will begin (and have begun) within this generation. Do not lose hope, *because*
2. Christ will be near to protect his church; *however,*
3. No one knows the exact time of his coming; *therefore,*
4. We must always be ready lest it catch us off guard.

In placing the prediction of calamities in the same context as the discourse on the Second Coming, the Eschatological Discourse expresses hope in the midst of impending trials rather than despair because of them. Jesus "predicts" calamities, which have been fulfilled, then speaks of his Second Coming, which has not. As the calamities came to pass as Jesus had "foretold," how much more will Jesus' promise to return in glory be fulfilled, whenever that event may come.

STUDY QUESTIONS

Judgment and the Second Coming of Christ

1. Which of St. Paul's letters has eschatology as the principal focus?
2. What are the apocalyptic themes found in the Gospels?
3. What about the historical setting in which the Gospels were composed would have influenced the writing of Jesus' Eschatological Discourse?
4. Can St. Paul's letters and the Gospels be considered apocalyptic literature? Why or why not?

5
THE BOOK OF REVELATION

INTRODUCTION AND BACKGROUND

The Book of Revelation is not a blueprint for what will happen at the end of the world. One must remember Christ's assurance to the apostles that no one knows when the end will come—not even the Son. Only the Father who is in heaven knows this. Therefore, to interpret Revelation in terms of the literal end of the world would be to undermine the words of Christ[1] as well as to distract ourselves from the dynamic richness of its message: the saving power of God. No one knows when the end will come. Therefore, one must not and cannot interpret Revelation in this way.

The Book of Revelation cannot be interpreted in physical terms. To do so would be to completely disregard the nature and purpose of apocalyptic literature. We cannot be looking for the sky to be rolled up like a scroll, or the sun to turn red, or one-third of the stars to fall from the sky. We cannot be looking for the beast to come up from the sea, the four riders of the Apocalypse to ride out of the sky, or the battle of Armageddon to occur at a particular time and place. Instead, we must look to the underlying spiritual message behind the Book of Revelation and the relevance of that message to Christian faith in Jesus Christ.

The meaning behind the images and the message behind the events are larger, more dynamic, more uplifting, and more hopeful than any literal event described by the book. To a person of faith, Revelation means much more than what is presented. It is a dynamic expression of something we already know and believe. To a person of faith, Revelation presents nothing new, but rather aims to inspire a sense of vigor in a faith that already exists—faith in the imminent victory of Christ.

The Book of Revelation does not predict specific future events. Rather it inspires hope for the future by interpreting a crisis of the present within the overall plan of God. Revelation speaks of a reality already in existence—the victory of Christ over evil—and applies it to the early church's experience of persecution. Christ's victory is the unchanging truth expressed in the book, which is universal to the people of God for all time. To the early Christians of the late first century AD, Revelation presented a conflict between two worlds—the world of Roman domination (earth, Babylon) and the world of heaven—with the heavenly world offered as an alternative to the Roman world. It inspires perseverance in the midst of conflict, assuring future victory and salvation for those who endure.

Who wrote the Book of Revelation? The author is mentioned in the very first verse. John was a common name in the ancient world. However, attempts to connect the name to a specific figure in history—not the least of which is the apostle John—are difficult. Some see John as a common holy man's name as in the case of the prophet Daniel. There are some similarities with the Gospel of John and its theology, such as the use of "Lamb" to symbolize Christ. There is, however, reference to other New Testament theologies. We learn from Revelation itself that John was a Christian with a reputation for being a prophet, he had experienced persecution for the faith, and he was known to the seven churches to whom Revelation is addressed.

Where does Revelation take place? In Revelation 1:9 John states that he is in exile on the island of Patmos, off the coast of Asia Minor on the southeastern part of the Aegean Sea. The messages at the beginning of Revelation are addressed to seven churches in the same general area. Some have called this region the cradle of New Testament literature. The Acts of the Apostles, the Johannine literature (the Gospel and letters attributed to an author named John, believed to be the "beloved disciple" of the Gospel of John), and St. Paul's missionary journeys are all centered on this area of the Roman Empire, which today is southwestern Turkey.

When was Revelation written? The book is dated around AD 95, toward the end of the reign of the emperor Domitian (AD 81–96). By this time, Roman forces had destroyed the Temple in Jerusalem (in AD 70), which resulted in much internal struggle within the Jewish community over identity—can we survive without the Temple? To the Christians, Rome came to be known as the second "Babylon" to destroy the Temple of Jerusalem.

The Christian community, which had originated as a sect within Judaism and still observed its customs, was formally expelled from the synagogues and from Judaism in AD 85. This resulted in an internal struggle within the Christian community over their own identity—can we survive without being part of Judaism? Under Roman rule one was expected to follow the Roman religion. Rome, however, had given a dispensation to the Jews and to any religion in existence at the time of the Roman conquest. While this did not include Christianity, the early Christians enjoyed this dispensation because they were considered a Jewish sect—Jesus, St. Peter, St. Paul, and the other apostles were all Jews. However, after their expulsion from Judaism, Christians were no longer considered Jews, and thus were no longer dispensed from Roman religion. As a result, Christianity became subject to persecution.

By the time Revelation was written the emperor Nero had persecuted the Christians for burning Rome. Other persecutions would later break out, such as those of emperors Domitian (AD 81–96) and Diocletian (AD 284–305), who have become known historically as persecutors of Christians. In addition, regional persecutions broke out throughout early Christian history that were not official empire-wide persecutions, but were products of the local region.

Why was the Book of Revelation written? Many of the symbols and cosmic occurrences of Revelation reflect the experience of persecution and the Christian's role in it.[2] The earthly struggle against persecution is portrayed as a heavenly struggle between the powers of good and evil. The Greek word for victory, *nikao*, which occurs twenty-one times in the New Testament, occurs fifteen times in the Book of Revelation alone. The Greek word for "conquer" occurs seventeen times, fifteen in regard to the conquest of evil.[3] To the Christians of the late first century AD, to whom and for whom the book was originally written, Revelation gives a heavenly perspective to the experience of early Christians. What is really happening? We participate in a heavenly liturgy, and are struggling in the heavenly struggle against Satan and his agents (Rome). The transcendent reality of the Book of Revelation is the heavenly struggle between good and evil in which the victory of Christ is imminent because it has already been won.

The Book of Revelation also addresses other issues of its time. The realities of complacency, making one prone to conforming to the unprincipled values of a surrounding society, are strongly addressed in the letters to the seven churches at the beginning of the book (Rev 2—3). The eating of meat sacrificed to idols (Rev 2:20) as an expression of giving in to false teaching was a particular travesty to first-century Christianity, as were heretical movements such as those of "Balaam" and the Nicolaitans (Rev 2:14–15), which would have been known to the churches of that time. However, the underlying issue of watering down one's faith in favor of the values of the surrounding culture remains a problem even for modern Christianity.[4] In this way, the Book of Revelation continues to speak to the church, both undergoing persecution and facing cultural values contrary to its teaching.

What is the Book of Revelation? Revelation is an apocalypse similar to other apocalypses with a systematic format to its presentation. There are strong liturgical elements in Revelation (see Fig. 7 on the next page). It begins in the context of liturgy (Rev 1:1–3), then sounds like a letter addressed to "the seven churches that are in Asia" (Rev 1:4). The book develops into a vision (Rev 1:9—22:9), returns to a letter (Rev 22:10–22), and concludes in the context of liturgy (Rev 22:17–20).

The themes of the Book of Revelation can be outlined as follows:

Chapters:

1	Prologue and greeting
2—3	Messages to the churches
4—5	The heavenly throne room
6—8	Opening of the scroll—the seven seals
9—11	The seven trumpets
12—13	The anti-Trinity (dragon and two beasts)
14	The companions of the Lamb and the harvest of the earth
15—16	The seven last plagues—the seven bowls

17—19 The fall of Babylon
20   The thousand-year reign of the King of kings
21—22 The new creation and epilogue

Overall the Book of Revelation comprises two cycles of visions following the greeting and the messages to the churches. The first cycle (4:1—11:19) covers the vision of the heavenly throne room, the cycle of the seven seals, and the cycle of the seven trumpets. The second cycle (12:1—22:5) covers the visions of the anti-Trinity, the harvest of the earth, the seven last plagues, the fall of Babylon, the thousand-year reign of the King of kings, and the new creation.

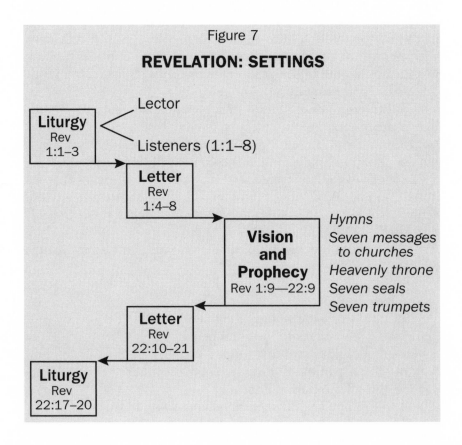

Figure 7

REVELATION: SETTINGS

SETTING THE STAGE FOR THE REVELATION

Revelation 1:1–3—The Prologue

Apocalypse is the first word of the Book of Revelation. It is the only time the word is used in the entire book, making note of the singular revelation. Hence, the apocalypse is not called the Book of Revelation*s*, a common error. There is only *one* revelation of the book—the victory of Christ.

The prologue presents the chain of voices and thereby introduces the key characters of the book—God, Jesus, the angel, John, and the servants of God. Jesus, having received the revelation from God, communicates it through the angel who interprets it to John, and ultimately to the servants. In short, the Book of Revelation is a message from Jesus to the servants.

Three key terms in the book are mentioned in the first three verses. In addition to *apocalypsis*, which is revealing that which is hidden, the term for witness, *martyria*—from which is derived the word *martyr*—occurs frequently in the Book of Revelation and throughout Johannine literature. *Martyria* gives witness to the salvation of Jesus, but also contains a legal reference, the weighing of evidence or a witness to the truth. The third key term introduced is *prophetia*, or prophecy, which refers to the message of the Book of Revelation. Here again, the word *prophecy* or *prophetic message* is singular, referring to the one revelation of the book. Prophecy is not necessarily used to mean a prediction of the future, but an interpretation of what is happening now.

Finally, the prologue contains the first of seven beatitudes— "Blessed is the one who reads aloud the words of the prophecy, and blessed are those who hear and who keep what is written in it" (v. 3). The blessings of beatitude contain the power of life, while curses contain the power of death. The blessings to the "one who reads" and "those who hear" suggest a setting in which people are gathered in groups to hear the message of Revelation read aloud. The setting, therefore, may have been liturgical.

The other six beatitudes are clustered in the second half of the Book of Revelation:

Rev 14:13—"Blessed are the dead who from now on die in the Lord."

Rev 16:15—"Blessed is the one who stays awake and is clothed."

Rev 19:9—"Blessed are those who are invited to the marriage supper of the Lamb."

Rev 20:6—"Blessed and holy are those who share in the first resurrection."

Rev 22:7—"Blessed is the one who keeps the words of the prophecy of this book."

Rev 22:14—"Blessed are those who wash their robes, so that they will have the right to the tree of life."

Revelation 22:7 repeats the beatitude of the prologue.

Revelation 1:4–8—The Greeting to the Churches

The Book of Revelation addresses seven churches. In Scripture the number 7 symbolizes the fullness of perfection. Therefore, the address to seven churches, while specific to particular communities, implies the fullness of the church as a whole. Thus John is writing to the entire church.

As the book continues to set the stage for the revelation, the author bestows grace and blessings on his listeners from the source of all grace and blessing. He evokes a triune God, but this trinity is a little different from the Trinity we are familiar with—Father, Son, and Holy Spirit. First, he refers to God as "him who is and who was and who is to come," an existence related to our understanding of time. Hence the focus is not only on God's existence, but also on the relationship between an eternal God and the world existing in time.

The seven spirits are referred to more than once in Revelation. One explanation for the sevenfold spirit (apparently referring to the Holy Spirit in this passage) is that in apocalyptic literature—as we saw in Daniel—people and groups have a heavenly host representing them in the heavenly conflict. Just as Michael was the champion of the Jews in Daniel, the seven spirits may refer to the seven churches being addressed. Each church has a presiding spirit that watches over and protects that particular community (Rev

1:20b). The concept of the sevenfold spirit may also have roots in Isaiah 11:2, which describes the spirit of the Lord as "a spirit of wisdom and of understanding, a spirit of counsel and of strength, a spirit of knowledge and of piety and his delight shall be the fear of the LORD." From this derives the basis of the sevenfold gifts of the Holy Spirit.[5]

Finally, grace and peace are bestowed from Jesus Christ, who is called "the faithful witness, the first born of the dead, and the ruler of the kings of the earth" (Rev 1:5). These references to Christ are seen in three New Testament traditions. *Faithful witness* is a term common to Johannine literature. Giving witness to the truth is a principal theme in John's Gospel, examples of which are found in the stories of the cure of the paralytic (John 5:1–15) and the cure of the man born blind (John 9). The beneficiary of the miracle gives testimony to the Pharisees. The other two terms used for Christ come from other early Christian traditions. St. Paul speaks of Christ as "the first born from the dead" (1 Cor 15:20; Col 1:18). *Ruler of the kings of earth* is a term common in the Synoptic tradition—the Gospels of Matthew, Mark, and Luke, and the Acts of the Apostles. (It is also one of the three issues addressed in the Book of Daniel.) This idea of universal rule also brings to mind the temptation of Jesus (Matt 4:8–9; Luke 4:5–7). The tempter's promise that Jesus refused is now achieved, not from the tempter, but by the triumph of the cross.

Verse 6 states our identity and relationship before God. Jesus has made us into a nation or kingdom that recognizes the real king and shares his kingly power. He has also made us into priests who offer worship and who know where true worship belongs—to the heavenly throne, not to the Roman throne. The image of the one coming on the clouds in verse 7 evokes a Baal image. While this is not as yet a storm theophany as we understand it from ancient Canaanite mythology, Baal is now replaced by God the Father.

Finally, God the Father speaks of three titles. As distinct from Jesus Christ, it is the first of only two times in the Book of Revelation in which the Father (or the "Lord God") is identified as the speaker. The other is Revelation 21:5–8. The "Lord God" describes himself using three principal descriptions. First, he is "the Alpha and the Omega." Alpha and Omega, the first and last letters of the Greek alphabet, give a sense of completion; they point both to creation (protology) and to the end times (eschatology). This title of Revelation 1:8 will be repeated by God in 21:6 and by the Son in 22:13, who takes his place on the heavenly throne and assumes the title to himself. At this point in Revelation, however, the Father holds the title. God the Father is also "the Lord God, who is and who was and who is to come," spanning all time and eternity. Finally, God is "the Almighty," with dominion over all things.

Revelation 1:9–20—The First Vision

The stage having been set, the characters introduced, and the greeting bestowed, John now steps forward to present his vision. Before addressing the churches individually John begins with a greeting that shows familiarity with the churches he is addressing. He is also familiar with their situations. A fellow servant with the other Christians, John shares three things with them. (1) He shares the distress or the tribulation, a familiar part of the apocalyptic scenario. (2) He shares the kingdom or the kingly reign, and expresses the belief that as Christians we already share in the kingdom of God, a reality of the present. (3) Finally, John shares the endurance, which includes patience and perseverance in trials. In this early stage of the revelation John seeks to uplift his listeners, who, like him, are suffering persecution. His message is the same for Christians of all ages. The reason we share distress is because we share the kingdom, which is at odds with the world. So let us endure the distress and share in the victory.

John sets his vision on the island of Patmos, in exile, "on the Lord's day" (Rev 1:10). This is distinct from the Jewish Sabbath (Saturday). As Christians we identify the "Lord's day" as Sunday. As the day of Christ's resurrection and a day of worship for Christians, the Lord's day has liturgical meaning that places the vision of John more securely in the context of liturgy. By suggesting that revelation is received in the context of worship, this attributes an importance to worship on the Lord's day.

John is instructed to write down his vision and to send it to seven churches specifically named (Rev 1:11). The seven locations to which John is instructed to send his vision were located in sequence along a major road in western Asia Minor. So it would have been easy to pass along the message from place to place.[6]

The phrase "one like the Son of Man" calls up the image of Daniel 7:13 in which one of that description is given dominion by God. The description of him in Revelation 1:13–16 echoes the image of Daniel 10:4–9. This person identifies himself as the "First and the Last." An echo of Isaiah 41:4, 44:6, and 48:12, the title of "the First and the Last" is one identified with God. His claim "I was dead, and see, I am alive forever and ever" and his mastery over death and the netherworld directly identifies this person as Jesus Christ. This title will be combined with the title "Alpha and Omega" at the conclusion of the book (Rev 22:13).

The seven lampstands among which the person walks are later described as symbolic of the seven churches to which Revelation is addressed. The seven stars in his right hand represent the "presiding spirits" over those churches (Rev 1:20). This is consistent with the themes of apocalyptic literature in that each church has a representative in the heavenly realm that serves as a champion or protector. Hence, each church has a presiding angel or a particular manifestation of the Holy Spirit watching over it.

Revelation 2–3—The Messages to the Churches

John communicates messages from Christ to the seven churches named in Revelation 1:11. The messages are in the form of prophetic speeches, and each begins with a prophetic commission—"To the angel of the church...write..." The command to "go" is replaced with a command to "write" since the author was confined to Patmos.[7] In the messages he comments on each church's difficult situation and urges endurance. The longest of these letters is to the church at Thyatira, the shortest to the church at Smyrna.

Each city has a particular characteristic. Ephesus, the first to be spoken to, was the capital city of the province. Smyrna, to whom the second and shortest of the letters was addressed, was a very famous city and considered the loveliest. Pergamum was at one time the capital city of the region and was still considered to be among the greatest or most famous. The city of Thyatira, which

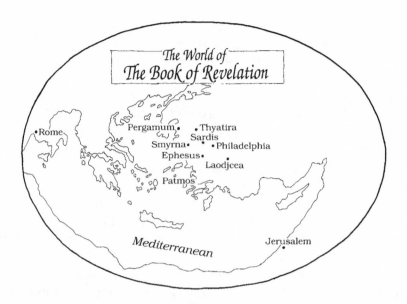

receives the longest of the letters, is by contrast the least important city in the province of Asia. Sardis was the oldest and most decayed city, considered a place of degradation. Philadelphia was among the youngest or freshest. Destroyed by an earthquake in AD 17, it had since been rebuilt. Finally, Laodicea, a wealthy commercial center, has the distinction among the seven of being the rejected city.

The letters follow similar patterns. A reference to Christ is taken from the vision at the beginning of Revelation (1:13–18). Praise to the individual church is offered as well as a reproach. Sometimes there is only one or the other: Smyrna and Philadelphia receive only praise while Sardis and Laodicea receive only a reproach. Sometimes there is both, as in the case of Ephesus, Pergamum, and Thyatira, which receive both praise and reproach. There is also a promise to or about the victor that foreshadows the events at the end of Revelation. The letter ends with an urging to heed what the Spirit says.

The problems that were faced by the churches can be categorized into three groups.

1. *The churches faced problems from outside the Christian community*—namely, the persecutions they were suffering at the hands of the Roman Empire and the Jewish community. As history bears wit-

ness, Roman society, culture, and worship was on a collision course with Christianity. In Revelation 2:13—the letter to Pergamum— John refers to "Satan's throne," thus foreshadowing later persecutions and perhaps recognizing Pergamum's former status as a local capital or its religious (albeit pagan) and cultural grandeur. In any case, persecutions had either begun or were imminent.

Since their expulsion from the synagogue, the Christian community had been alienated from the Jewish community. Since Christians expelled from the synagogue no longer enjoyed an exemption from the observance of Roman religion, they were exposed to persecution by the Roman Empire. "Satan's assembly" in the letter to Smyrna (Rev 2:9) refers to the protected status of the Jews under the Roman system. While sounding extremely anti-Semitic, the mention of "self-styled Jews" or "those who say that they are Jews and are not, but are a synagogue of Satan" would have reflected the conflict between Christians and Jews in Smyrna similar to that between the Jews and the community of Qumran. Such an enmity would not have condemned all Jews, but would have risen out of great bitterness over those Jews who antagonize Christianity while enjoying protection under the Roman system. Hence, in the view of Revelation's author they are not true Jews but only claim to be such. The act of expelling Christians from the synagogue and exposing them to persecution by Rome (Satan's throne) would naturally be seen as an act of the evil one—Satan.

2. *The churches faced internal problems*—the false teachings and heresy that circulated within the community. The letter to Pergamum reproaches the city for harboring false teachers (Rev 2:14). Balaam is a figure from Old Testament tradition. He appears in Numbers 22—24 in a positive light. Balak, the king of Moab, calls upon Balaam to curse the Israelites. Instead, Balaam utters a series of blessings according to the command of God. In Numbers 31:16, however, Balaam is presented in a negative light as one who leads Israel into sin. Revelation refers to this negative tradition when speaking of false teachers.

Revelation 2:6 and 2:15 mention a group called the Nicolaitans. While some scholars have made educated guesses as to the identity of the Nicolaitans, no one knows for sure who or what they were.

From Revelation's messages to Ephesus and Pergamum, however, it is clear that they promote illicit and compromising behavior.

The letter to Thyatira refers to Jezebel (Rev 2:20), the most notorious queen in Hebrew history. A Phoenician princess and wife to King Ahab in the northern kingdom of Israel, Jezebel was independent of the Mosaic covenant. Jezebel, having encouraged the worship of Baal throughout the northern kingdom, represents the temptation to forsake Yahweh and worship false gods. She became the nemesis of the prophet Elijah and sought to have him killed. Elijah stood firm in the face of her persecution. Seduction, lewdness, and playing the harlot refer to the selling of oneself to idolatry. Eating food sacrificed to idols is a gesture that expresses support of idol worship.

3. *The churches faced the problem of lukewarmness.* In some places Christianity was losing its zeal. Choices and problems were not being faced as clearly or as faithfully as they should have been. With complacency came the tendency to dull the fire of the Spirit. Laodicea is highly criticized for this, and this church receives the strongest message: "So because you are lukewarm, and neither cold nor hot, I am about to spit you out of my mouth" (Rev 3:16).

Each of the seven churches is promised a share in Christ's victory, and each of the promised gifts foreshadows the end of the Book of Revelation when the victory is celebrated (see Fig. 8 on the next page). To Ephesus is promised eating from the tree of life in the heavenly paradise (Rev 2:7). The tree of life in the Garden of Eden was barred to Adam and Eve after they ate of the tree of knowledge. Now it is promised to the victor. It also foreshadows the trees of life that will grow in the New Jerusalem (Rev 22:2). To Smyrna is promised the crown of life and preservation from the second death (2:10–11), foreshadowing the death suffered by the idol-worshippers and deceivers who will be cast into the fiery pool of burning sulfur (Rev 21:8).

Pergamum is promised the hidden manna and a white stone on which is inscribed a new name (Rev 2:17). The hidden manna calls to mind the food provided by God to the children of Israel as they passed through the desert after the Exodus. Various suggestions have been offered as to the meaning of the white stone. The new name, however, calls to mind the practice in Old Testament

Figure 8

PROMISES TO THE CHURCHES: REV 2—3		
Church Addressed	Promises **"to everyone who conquers…"**	Foreshadowing the New Creation and the New Jerusalem
Ephesus	*"permission to eat from the tree of life that is in the paradise of God."*—2:7	*"On either side of the river is the tree of life."*—22:2
Smyrna	*"will not be harmed by the second death."*—2:11	*"their place will be in the lake that burns with fire and sulfur, which is the second death."*—21:8
Pergamum	*"a white stone, and on the white stone is written a new name."*—2:17	*"his name will be on their foreheads."* —22:4
Thyatira	*"authority over the nations."*—2:26	*"kings of the earth will bring their glory into it."* —21:24
Sardis	*"will be clothed like them in white robes, and I will not blot your name out of the book of life."*—3:5	*"only those who are written in the Lamb's book of life."*—21:27
Philadelphia	*"I will make you a pillar in the temple of my God."*—3:12	*"its temple is the Lord God the Almighty and the Lamb."*—21:22
Laodicea	*"I will give a place with me on my throne."* —3:21	*"they will reign forever and ever."* —22:5

history of renaming those who enjoy a new status with God. Abram was renamed Abraham because God made him the father of nations (Gen 17:5). Jacob was renamed Israel because he had wrestled with a divine being and prevailed (Gen 32:29). Isaiah 62:2 speaks of a promise given by God in which Israel "shall be called by a new name." The promise of a new name is also proposed to be the name of Christ himself, foreshadowing Revelation 22:4, in which the servants bear his name on their foreheads.

Thyatira is promised judgment over the nations (Rev 2:26), an echo of Psalm 2:8–9, in which the Messiah-king is promised such authority. It is a foreshadowing of the light of the Lamb in Revelation 21:24 by which all the nations will walk. Sardis is promised white garments and their name in the book of life (Rev 3:5). This foreshadows the book of the living kept by the Lamb in which are inscribed the names of those who will be permitted to enter the New Jerusalem (Rev 21:27). The white garments are worn by the martyrs (Rev 6:11) and by those who have washed their robes in the blood of the Lamb (Rev 7:9, 14). To Philadelphia is promised that the victor shall be made a pillar in the temple of God (Rev 3:12), which alludes to the rebuilding of the city. Just as Philadelphia had been rebuilt after the earthquake of AD 17, the victor shall become a pillar in the temple of the New Jerusalem (Rev 21:7).

The church of Laodicea, which receives the harshest message, is promised close intimacy with Christ. They are even reminded that such strong reproach is done out of love (Rev 3:19). The promise of enjoying a place at Christ's table and upon his throne (Rev 3:20–21) implies a table fellowship with him in the banquet of heaven as the apostles shared at the Last Supper. It also indicates a sharing in Christ's power, which is later assured to those who suffered martyrdom for the faith (Rev 20:4–6) and to those servants who enter the New Jerusalem (Rev 22:3–5).

THE HEAVENLY THRONE ROOM

Throughout the Book of Revelation the scene shifts back and forth between heaven and earth. The visions related by John occur in cycles that include a basic pattern of *persecution, judgment,* and *salvation.* While there are still a number of events to come before the revelation reaches completion, the rest of the book spells out in more detail the spirit and sentiment expressed in the opening sections— the reality of persecution and the virtue of endurance so as to see salvation.

In Matthew 16:18 Jesus declares Peter to be the rock upon which he will build his church and assures Peter that "the gates of hell shall not prevail against it." What is invoked is not a passive church or the passive forces of good. Rather the forces of good are actively on the attack against the forces of evil. The gates of hell shall not prevail against heaven's assault on them, and the church is the instrument of that assault against evil.

The same is true in the Book of Revelation. The Christian church of the first century AD was either under or in danger of persecution at the hands of the Roman Empire. The imagery of Revelation 6—11 describes heaven taking the initiative in its defense of the church against the forces of persecution. Once the heavenly assault is completed and the Lord and his anointed take possession of the kingdom of earth, the evil forces of hell will emerge in Revelation 12—13 to do battle against the heavenly realm. Two champions will be called upon. The church will call upon the heavenly throne to do battle on its behalf. The earthly realm of evil will call upon the dragon and the beasts to do battle against the forces of good. However, it is the heavenly realm that takes the initiative by going on the assault. In the end, it is the heavenly realm fighting for the church that wins out over the forces of evil, death, and idolatry. As Jesus assured Peter, the gates of hell do not prevail.

Revelation 4—The Vision of the Heavenly Throne Room

The vision that follows the messages to the churches and the context in which it is presented is the heart of the Book of Revelation. There is a dramatic change of scene and style. Revelation 3:20, "I am standing at the door, knocking," links the messages to the experience of the heavenly throne room. (The word for "throne" occurs sixteen times in chapters 4 and 5; forty-six times in the entire book. There is a contrast between the thrones of God/the Lamb and the Devil/beast.)

In chapter 4 John passes from earth to heaven through the open door and gets to witness a heavenly perspective on what is going on below. The sense of time changes in that there is a movement from what must happen "soon" (Rev 1:1) to what must happen "in time to come" or "afterward" (Rev 4:1). The vision of the throne room is seen in the context of worship, filled with music and praise. The imagery becomes more symbolic, dramatic, and bizarre.

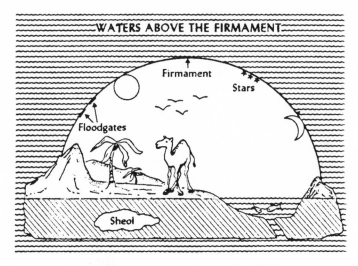

An artist's portrayal of the universe as understood by the ancient Semitic world.

To understand the places described, as well as the passage from earth to heaven, it is necessary to understand the ancient Hebrew view of the world. Just as the people of fifteenth-century Europe believed the world was flat, and just as some of the cultures of ancient Asia believed the earth was on the back of a tortoise, the Hebrews too had a vision of the structure of the earth and the cosmos. The Hebrews envisioned the dry land of the earth resting on pillars that held the land above the abyss of the sea. The waters of the sea were thought to extend above the sky. In the firmament of the sky were the sun, moon, stars, and all the celestial bodies. The water was kept above the firmament by floodgates, which remained shut (see Gen 7:11). Above these waters was the heavenly seat of divinity. In chapter 4 of Revelation John is caught up to that heavenly realm.

The first thing John sees is the throne itself, surrounded by a brilliant rainbow upon which is One whose appearance is like that of a gem (Rev 4:2–3). Surrounding the throne are twenty-four elders. Some believe that their number represents the Old and New Israel—the twelve tribes of Israel and the twelve apostles. This would link the present Christian community founded on the apostles with their heritage in the Jewish community founded upon the tribes. In Babylonian mythology and astrology there were twenty-four gods encompassed in the stars, half to the north and half to the south. If this is the inspiration of the image of the elders around the throne, then their presence in the vision could symbolize the cosmic order. The image of the elders around the throne may also have its inspiration in the Roman custom by which senators, men of rank, advisors, or friends would surround the emperor to bear witness when he heard cases.[8] The elders eventually offer worship to the One seated on the throne who holds dominion over all.

The thunder and lightning coming forth from the throne (Rev 4:5) echo the traditional image of storm theophany, which accompanies the manifestation of God. John also sees seven flaming torches, which represent the seven spirits of God. The floor around the throne, "a sea of glass like crystal" (Rev 4:6), hearkens back to the ancient Hebrew view of the world and the heavenly realm. The waters above the firmament were below the heavenly seat of divinity. These waters are described as the floor beneath the heavenly throne, and are calm, smooth, and clear.

Finally, surrounding the throne itself, John sees the four living creatures who day and night sing God's praises (Rev 4:6b–8)—a lion, an ox, a man, and an eagle. Like the four creatures of Daniel 7 these creatures are bizarre in their appearance. They are covered with eyes, front and back, inside and out, and each has six wings. They also appear to have particular authority within the worship itself. They are the closest to the throne and "whenever [they] give glory and honor and thanks to the one who is seated on the throne…the

The Four Living Creatures
Symbolizing the Man, the Lion, the Ox, and the Eagle, crudely depicted.

twenty-four elders fall before the one…and worship the one who lives forever and ever." The elders cast their crowns before the throne and join in singing praise, taking their cue from the four living creatures (Rev 4:9–10). This image is borrowed by the author of the popular hymn "Holy, Holy, Holy" in the lines "Holy, holy, holy! / All the saints adore thee, / Casting down their golden crowns around the glassy sea."

These creatures are traditionally identified as symbols of the four evangelists—Matthew (man), Mark (lion), Luke (ox), and John (eagle). However, it is unlikely that the author of Revelation had this in mind, since the contents of the New Testament as we know it, and thus the decision to include these four Gospels, were not finalized until much later. The motifs of the four living creatures may have been borrowed from Ezekiel 1:10 and may be of Babylonian origin. Some see in the four living creatures a symbolic representation of all creatures in creation. The lion is popularly known as the king of beasts, the supreme among animals. The ox is the strongest of the cattle, the beasts of burden, or any domesticated animal—hence, the phrase "strong as an ox." Humanity is the dominant being on the earth. The eagle would be considered dominant among birds of the air. Therefore, the four living creatures may represent all creatures on the earth participating in the heavenly worship. Indeed it is a fundamental idea that anything that fulfills the basic function for which it was created is praising God. Such is the sentiment behind the popular hymn: "All creatures of our God and king, / lift up your voice, and with us sing, / Alleluia, Alleluia." Whatever the interpretation, whether intended by the author or developed over time and tradition, the four living creatures are clearly part of the imagery of heaven and have an important place in the worship of God.

Revelation 5—The Lamb That Was Slain

Chapter 5 continues the description of the heavenly throne room. The scroll sealed with the seven seals becomes the focus of the entire chapter. An angel asks who is worthy to open the scroll, and John weeps bitterly because no one is found. Finally, the Lamb is seen for the first time and is declared to be worthy.

The Lamb, like the living creatures, has a bizarre appearance. First of all, the Lamb has been slain, referring to the crucified Christ. The marks of its being slain are apparently visible to John even in the heavenly realm. In addition, it has seven horns and seven eyes that symbolize perfect power/honor and perfect sight. The seven eyes as "the seven spirits of God sent out into all the earth" (Rev 5:6) echo Zechariah 4:10, in which the seven lamps are identified as the eyes of God that range over the world.

The Lamb's description as "the Lion of the tribe of Judah, the Root of David" (Rev 5:5) has messianic implications pertaining to Christ. The Lion of Judah hearkens back to Jacob's testimony before his death in Genesis 49:9, when he likens his son Judah to a lion's whelp. The Root of David echoes Isaiah 11:1, which predicts that the shoot from the stump of Jesse will bring forth the messianic reign of peace. Both Judah and David are direct ancestors of Christ, and they symbolize power and kingly dignity. The Lamb who was slain, however, appears as a contrasting image of lowliness and sacrifice.

Worship is extended to the Lamb, as are the prayers of God's holy people (Rev 5:8). This prayer has three sections, and in each section more worshipers join in the chorus. First, the elders and the living creatures fall down before the Lamb. They sing a new hymn declaring the Lamb's worthiness because it has been slain; it has purchased all people for God, making them "a kingdom and priests serving our God" who "will reign on earth" (Rev 5:8–10). This indicates a sharing of power (kings) and worship (priests). In the second section, many angels join in the hymn. The Lamb is declared worthy not only to open the scroll but also to "receive power and wealth and wisdom and might and honor and glory and blessing" (Rev 5:12)—all godly qualities. The song of praise grows louder and louder in the third section as John describes more and more people joining in the hymn until finally he hears "every creature in heaven and on earth and under the earth and in the sea, and all that is in them, singing" (Rev 5:13) in adoration of Christ, the Lamb.

Chapter 5 ends with this hymn extending power, honor, and praise to the Lamb now seated on the throne. The hymn acknowledges that the Lamb (Jesus) is God and that we (the victor) will sit with him on the throne (as in Rev 3:21). Just as the Lamb won vic-

Figure 9

OPENING THE SCROLL: REV 6:1—8:2		
Seals 1–4	Social Collapse	(Earth)
Seal 5	Reflects and Recollects Persecutions	(Heaven)
Seal 6	Cosmic Collapse	(Earth)
	(Interlude)	(Heaven)
Seal 7	Great Silence	(Heaven)

tory through dying, so the faithful—under persecution—win victory through martyrdom.

THE HEAVENLY INTERVENTION

Now that the reality of the heavenly realm has been established, we enter into another phase of Revelation, when heaven itself intercedes for the persecuted church. The scroll sealed with seven seals is now opened. With the peeling of each seal the events of the church's experience are symbolically interpreted from different angles and the intervention of the heavenly realm is unleashed. The first four seals are opened in quick succession, the last three seals at a slower pace. The sequence begins with a collapse of the social order and reaches a climax with the collapse of the cosmic order (see Fig. 9 above).

Revelation 6—7—The Opening of the Scroll

As each of the **first four seals** is opened, one of the Four Horsemen of the Apocalypse is called forth. The four horses upon which they ride are of different colors: white, red, black, and (sickly) green (Rev 6:1–8a). The riders have traditionally symbolized the ravages of destruction and the effects of war—conquest (white), bloodshed (red), famine (black), and pestilence (green), all ending in Death, the rider of the final horse. They are given authority to ravage one-quarter of the earth. Revelation 6:8 summarizes the effect of the first four seals—death by sword, famine, and plague. With the horsemen comes the breakdown of the social order, which is the result of any war or conquest. The image of

84

these four riders, taken from common imagery of the time, projects to the future the hope of eventual conquest of the persecuting Roman Empire.

The first rider, who rides forth at the breaking of the first seal, is on a white horse, a common Roman symbol for victory. When a Roman general returned after a great triumph and enjoyed the honor of a victory parade, he would ride in a chariot drawn by white horses. The first rider is also carrying a bow. This is commonly interpreted to symbolize the Parthians, Rome's strongest rival on the eastern frontier of the Roman Empire—the Tigris/Euphrates region. The people of the first-century Roman Empire were already aware of the menace of the barbarians—the Vandals, Huns, and Goths—who would eventually cause the empire to collapse. To a Jew or Christian living in Palestine, the Parthians would appear as champions against the dominance of the Roman military. Imagery of the Parthians will appear again in Revelation 9:13–19 and in Revelation 17. Hence, in the mindset of a first-century Christian, the ride of the four horsemen would be analogous to the collapse and ultimate death of Roman society.

With the breaking of the **fifth seal** the focus shifts from earth back to the heavenly realm. Since the second Temple had been destroyed in AD 70 and an earthly altar no longer existed, Revelation most likely refers to an altar in heaven. It also serves as a heavenly counterpart to the altar of the Temple that was destroyed. The image of the heavenly altar will be repeated in Revelation 8:3 and 14:18.

The vision of the fifth seal is one of persecution. John notes that under the heavenly altar are the spirits of the martyrs who died for the faith (Rev 6:9). From beneath the altar the souls of the martyrs cry out for their blood to be avenged. The cry for judgment and vindication is typical of lamentation: "how long will it be…" (Rev 6:10) (see also Ps 79:5–10). This type of prayer also reflects the honor-shame culture common in the ancient world. In such prayers of lamentation the psalmist calls upon the honor of God's name. Vindication is granted "for of the glory of your name" (Ps 79:9). With the destruction of Jerusalem and the persecution of God's people Yahweh again looks bad. After all, what kind of an all-powerful God would allow his chosen people, Christian or Jewish, to suffer conquest, destruction, and persecution? God's name must be vindicated and restored to honor. Hence the martyrs' prayers of lamentation call upon God for vengeance and judgment upon their persecutors not only for their sake, but also for the sake of God's honor and the honor of God's promise to those who believe in him.

The answer to the martyrs' call is unsettling. They are told to "rest a little longer, until the number would be complete both of their fellow servants and of their brothers and sisters, who were soon to be killed" (Rev 6:11). This is consistent with the promise of Jesus that the faithful will suffer persecution and martyrdom. In Matthew 10:17 Jesus says that others "will hand you over to councils and flog you in their synagogues," and later in Matthew 24:9 Jesus states, "they will hand you over to torture and kill you." Similar statements are found in Mark 13:9–13 and Luke 21:12. Therefore, the answer given to the lamentation of the martyrs is that more are to die for the faith. Their deaths cannot be avenged until the predetermined number has been killed. As hopeless as it appears, it is a subtly comforting, albeit very disquieting, reminder that when all is said and done, it is God who is ultimately in control over the church's experience.

With the breaking of the **sixth seal** the focus shifts back to earth and is a vision of judgment. Whereas the first four seals ushered in social collapse with the coming of war and its effects, the sixth seal ushers in the collapse of the cosmic order. The cosmic collapse can be seen as the heavenly response to the lament of the martyrs. The juxtaposition of the two visions suggests that the destruction is vengeance for the martyrs' death. The cry of those who suffer the destruction (Rev 6:16) further suggests that the disasters are the punishment for those who persecuted the followers of the Lamb.

The Lamb's wrath is described as universal, affecting all people of all social classes (Rev 6:15). Here again, heaven takes the initiative in protecting the faithful who suffer persecution and death by those who reject the Lamb. However, the image of such a violent wrath coming from a gentle Lamb is a paradox. We do not readily associate destruction and wrath with a lamb. The implication may be that God's wrath is one of love; God is not out to destroy in anger, but to save out of love. Those he saves are those who cry out for vindication and justice.

The events that occur at the breaking of the sixth seal are nothing new to apocalyptic literature. The collapse of the cosmos was an image very familiar to Jewish readers, who associated such events with the Day of the Lord. It would be a day when judgment would come to their enemies, and vindication would be given to those who remained faithful. Although some people seek to identify the events of the sixth seal with occurrences of our own time, they are not to be taken literally. Rather, they are traditional apocalyptic images. Even Christ himself uses such imagery in the Gospels when he speaks of the day when the Son of man returns. In Matthew Jesus speaks of earthquakes (24:7) and says that "the sun will be darkened, and the moon will not give its light, and the stars will fall from the sky, and the powers of the heavens will be shaken" (24:29; see also Mark 13:24 and Luke 21:25a).

The apocalyptic images describing the cosmic collapse that accompanies the breaking of the sixth seal begin with a violent earthquake (Rev 6:12). This is common, especially in Hebrew prophetic literature. For example, Ezekiel's prophecy against Gog includes a "great shaking upon the land of Israel" (38:18), and Joel 2:10 speaks of the Day of the Lord as a time when "the earth trembles and the heavens shake." Second, there is the darkening of the sun and moon (Rev 6:12b), an image found in Joel 2:10b, 3:4, and 3:15a.[9] Amos 8:9 speaks of the sun setting at midday and the earth being covered in darkness. The cosmic collapse continues with the falling of the stars and the folding up of the heavens (Rev 6:13–14), imagery also seen in Isaiah 34:4. Finally, the mountains and islands are uprooted (Rev 6:14b). In short, the cosmic order comes to an end with the opening of the sixth seal. Creation is undone and all things return to the chaos that existed before creation.

An **interlude** precedes the breaking of the seventh seal. Returning the focus to the heavenly realm, John sees a vision that expresses the theme of salvation, capping the threefold theme that recurs throughout the book—persecution (seal 5), judgment (seal 6), and salvation (interlude). The interlude consists of two visions of vast crowds, one of a specific number (Rev 7:1–8), the other of an uncountable multitude (Rev 7:9–17).

The first vision (Rev 7:1–8) begins when John sees four angels standing at the corners of the earth, holding back the four winds of destruction. The angels hold in check the instruments of punishment until the servants of God have been identified with the imprint of the seal of the living God. Another angel ascends from the east "having the seal of the living God." This protection of God's servants from the ravages of destruction is repeated in Revelation 9:4, when those sealed are spared the plague of locusts. This symbolic sealing reflects the Passover event, when the houses marked or sealed with the blood of the lamb survived the plague upon the first born (Exod 12:7, 13) and also echoes Ezekiel 9:4, in which those who did not give in to idolatry but groaned over its abominations are marked on their foreheads with an *X*. In the same way those sealed with the seal of the living God will survive the great destruction to come. The seal to be used is a brand or mark indicating that one belongs to God. In Revelation 7 the image of the mark is not clearly identified or described beyond being called the "seal of the living God."

The twelve tribes of Israel divide those who are marked. The tribes are named one by one, beginning with the tribe of Judah, from which emerged the Messiah. The number of people from each tribe adds up to a final tally of "one hundred forty-four thousand" marked with the seal of the living God (Rev 7:4). Does this mean that the 144,000 are exclusively Jews? The specific number of 144,000 indicates a sense of being chosen and the division of 12,000 from each tribe intensifies this sense. However, neither the exact number nor the allusion to the tribes of Israel should be taken literally. Considering Revelation's mention of "self-styled Jews" (Rev 2:9), this may refer to those considered to be true Jews.[10]

The division of the twelve tribes differs, however, from the traditional division found in the Old Testament, particularly in Numbers 1:5–15. Of the original twelve sons of Jacob from whom developed the twelve tribes, Joseph and Levi are not included, nor were they given a portion of the Promised Land. Rather Joseph's sons Manasseh and Ephraim become two of the twelve tribes. The Levites are likewise not counted among the tribes because they developed into the priestly class of Israel who performed the worship and sacrificial functions for all of the tribes, and eventually for the Temple. In the listing of Revelation 7:5–8, however, both Joseph and Levi are included, while Ephraim and Dan are excluded.

Ephraim and Dan were among the ten tribes that broke away from the southern kingdom and from Jerusalem in 922 BC. Samaria, in the province of Ephraim, became the capital city of the northern kingdom and a rival capital to Jerusalem. Ephraim's exclusion in Revelation may have to do with animosity surrounding the schism.

From the testimony given by Jacob in Genesis 49:16–17 Dan is likened to "a snake by the roadside…that bites the horse's heels so that its rider falls backward" (Gen 49:17). If this is meant to echo the serpent that tempted Eve in the Garden of Eden, then Dan becomes associated with sin and idolatry. Eventually Dan came to be considered the tribe from which would emerge a great enemy (Jer 8:16).[11] Christian tradition would later maintain that the anti-Christ would come from the tribe of Dan. The third-century theologian Hippolytus of Rome contrasted the anti-Christ born from the tribe of Dan to the Christ born of the tribe of Judah (*Concerning Antichrist*, 14).[12]

The second vision of the interlude (Rev 7:9–17) is that of an uncountable multitude "from every nation, from all tribes and peoples and languages" who stand before the throne and the Lamb. Unlike the group in the previous vision, which was meticulously counted by tribe and totaled to 144,000, this crowd is so vast as to be uncountable. They are dressed in white and hold palm branches, symbols of joy and victory. They are joined by the angels, the elders, and the four living creatures in a song of praise (Rev 7:9–12). This scene appears to mirror the praise in Revelation 5:13.

As is common in apocalyptic literature, an interpretation of the second vision is given to John by one of the elders. The imagery of their robes being washed white in the blood of the Lamb implies victory and purity through martyrdom. However, it may not mean such in a universal sense. The imagery may also reflect the uncountable multitude of those who have been redeemed by the blood of Christ's one sacrifice on the cross, a sacrifice that won for them eternal peace and salvation, expressed in the hymn that concludes the vision (Rev 7:15–17).

Figure 10

REVELATION 7—INTERPRETATIONS	
144,000 (Rev 7:4)	**Multitude** (Rev 7:9)
Faithful followers of the Mosaic covenant (Jews)	*Faithful followers of Christ (Christians)*
Jewish converts to Christianity	*Gentile converts to Christianity*
Holy men and women of the Old Testament	*Followers of Christ*
Church as the heir to the continuation of Israel	*Church reaching out to all nations*
Christians on earth (church militant)	*Faithful departed in heaven (church triumphant)*

Various suggestions have been put forth as to the meaning of this vision and the distinction between the uncountable multitude and the 144,000 (see Fig. 10 above).[13]

Revelation 8—9—The Silence and the Trumpets

Following the heavenly interlude the **seventh seal** is finally broken at the beginning of chapter 8. The scroll can now be opened and the judgment read! But this is not what happens. After the buildup of social collapse (seals 1–4), the cry of the martyrs (seal 5), the cosmic collapse (seal 6), and the sealing of the thousands in preparation for the tribulation, heaven meets the seventh seal with complete silence for a half hour (Rev 8:1).

During this silence two things are described. First, the seven angels are given seven trumpets, but do not as yet blow them. Second, another angel is seen holding a golden censer, the smoke of which rises up to God along with the prayers of the people. These prayers on the altar (now described as golden) call to mind the spirits of the martyrs below the altar, which cried out to God for justice at the breaking of the fifth seal. After taking burning coals from the heavenly altar, the angel hurls the censer to earth amid thunder and lightning and the trembling of the earth.

The vision of the seven angels, the seven trumpets, and the angel with the censer has strong liturgical elements that mirror on a smaller scale the prelude to the cycle of the seals. With the inclusion of the altar and the prayers rising before God the series of revelations continue to be set in the context of liturgy and worship.

There has been debate as to the significance of the heavenly silence. Some have suggested that the silence was necessary for the prayers offered with the incense to be heard by God. In this powerful illustration all activity in heaven comes to a halt so that the prayers of the holy ones may be heard. Others note that the breaking of the seventh seal brings about the entire cycle of the trumpets as a single, sevenfold calamity (Rev 8:1–2). Still others see the silence as a transition period linking the cycle of the seals with the cycle of the trumpets that affords a moment of preparation before the next events occur. In any case, the silence serves to build a dramatic anticipation for what is to follow. The uneven length of time (a half hour) further indicates this period as more a time of anticipation than one of rest and fulfillment. The anticipation grows in intensity with an entire verse dedicated to the angels preparing to blow the trumpets (Rev 8:6).

The blowing of the seven trumpets follows a pattern similar to that of the breaking of the seven seals. The first four are blown in quick succession, almost as a group. The next two are blown at a slower pace. Finally, there is an interlude of two visions before the seventh trumpet is blown.

With the blowing of the **first four trumpets** the effect on the earth grows in intensity. Whereas seals 1–4 and the four riders of the Apocalypse affected one-quarter of the earth, the trumpets affect one-third of the earth (see Fig. 11 on the next page).

There is a reversal of order in the effect of the trumpets compared to those of the seals. Whereas the cycle of the seals begins with social upheaval through war and destruction (seals 1–4) and ends in cosmic collapse (seal 6), the reverse is the case with the trumpets. Cosmic collapse begins the cycle with the first four trumpets. Social collapse comes with the sixth trumpet, described in a symbolic invasion by the Parthians. In addition, the fifth trumpet may be an answer to the fifth seal insofar as the vindication called for by the martyrs beneath the heavenly altar (seal 5) is

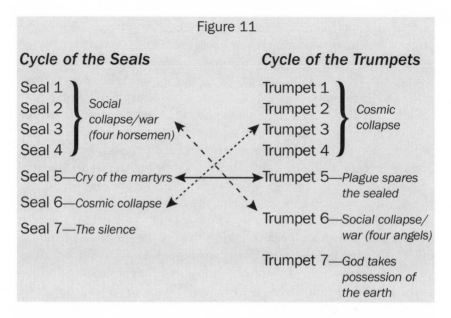

Figure 11

Cycle of the Seals

Seal 1
Seal 2 } Social
Seal 3 } collapse/war
Seal 4 } (four horsemen)

Seal 5—Cry of the martyrs

Seal 6—Cosmic collapse

Seal 7—The silence

Cycle of the Trumpets

Trumpet 1
Trumpet 2 } Cosmic
Trumpet 3 } collapse
Trumpet 4

Trumpet 5—Plague spares
the sealed

Trumpet 6—Social collapse/
war (four angels)

Trumpet 7—God takes
possession of
the earth

now carried out. With the blowing of the fifth trumpet, a plague of locusts affects those who do not have the seal of God, but spares those who do.

The cosmic effects of the first four trumpets are somewhat analogous to images from the Old Testament. The first two plagues that accompany the first two trumpets parallel two of the plagues upon Egypt in the Book of Exodus. However, where the plagues of the Exodus affected only Egypt, the plagues of the trumpets affect a much wider territory—one-third of the earth.

With the first trumpet comes a plague of hail mixed with fire (Rev 8:7). This recalls the seventh plague, when "fire came down on the earth. And the LORD rained hail on the land of Egypt" (Exod 9:23b). In addition to causing a huge mountain to be cast into the sea, the second trumpet results in one-third of the sea turning to blood, killing one-third of its creatures and wrecking one-third of the ships (Rev 8:8–9). This recalls the first plague upon Egypt, when the river turned to blood (Exod 7:14–24).

The third and fourth trumpets recall imagery from the prophets. With the third trumpet comes a plague similar to that in Jeremiah 9:12–16 in which God punishes those who succumb to idolatry by polluting their food and drinking water with wormwood (Rev 8:10–11). The fourth trumpet brings about darkness by affecting the sun, the moon, and the stars (Rev 8:12). While this may parallel the plague of darkness inflicted upon Egypt (Exod 10:22–23a) it is closer in imagery to Joel 4:15 and Amos 8:9.

With three trumpets yet to be blown, an eagle is seen flying and crying out an exclamation of doom. The triple enunciation of "woe" contrasts with the four living creatures of Revelation 4:8, who sang a triple "holy" to honor the Lord. The three woes characterize the final three trumpets and the plagues that they will bring about.

> **First Woe**—Rev 9:12—fifth trumpet (locust plague)
> **Second Woe**—Rev 11:14—after the sixth trumpet (vengeance for the witnesses)
> **Third Woe**—Rev 11:18a—seventh trumpet (judgment/wrath against the nations)

When the **fifth trumpet** is blown John sees a star falling from the sky and unlocking the abyss (Rev 9:1). In the ancient world the stars were understood to be representations of divinity. The Jews saw the stars as representing angels or spirits, as is seen in the beginning of Revelation (1:20b). The abyss was considered the place where Satan and the fallen angels were kept. The image, therefore, of a falling star would normally represent a fallen angel. However, since this star is given the key to the shaft of the abyss it does not mean that the act is one of rebellion. Rather it is part of God's plan.[14] From the unlocked abyss emerges smoke from which come locusts to do harm only to those who do not have the seal of God on their foreheads. This recalls the eighth plague on Egypt (Exod 13—15), although, unlike the eighth plague, these locusts are commanded not to ravage the land. This is noted as the first of the three woes.

Like the four beasts of Daniel 7 and the four living creatures of Revelation 4, the locusts, too, have a grotesque appearance—horses with men's faces, women's hair, teeth of lions, wings and stingers like scorpions. They are described in terms of military imagery—equipped for war, gold crowns, iron breastplates, and the roar of many chariots charging into battle (Rev 9:7–10). The name of the angel in charge of the abyss, Abaddon or "destruction," indicates an unleashing of the powers of chaos and evil during the end times. The inclusion of military imagery recalls the imagery of the first seal with its subsequent rider (Rev 6:2) and is continued in greater detail with the blowing of the next trumpet.

With the blowing of the **sixth trumpet,** four angels tied on the banks of the Euphrates are unleashed to destroy one-third of humanity (Rev 9:14–15). Unlike the locusts these troops are given permission to kill. The location in the east and at the Euphrates, and the mention of a great number of cavalry troops (two hundred million) calls to mind—as did the first seal—the empires of that region and the current threat of the Parthian Empire. Here, however, the imagery is of supernatural beings that carry out the divine wrath on the wicked. Again the images are dynamic and bizarre. The horses have heads of lions and breathe smoke, sulphur, and fire (Rev 9:17–18).

The golden altar of Revelation 9:13 is the same altar from under which came the lament of the martyrs (Rev 6:9) and from which rose the incense and the prayers of God's holy ones (Rev 8:3–5). Its appearance here links the plague of the sixth trumpet with the prayers of the holy ones and the lament of the martyrs. It further reinforces the impression that these plagues represent God's punishment on those who mistreated God's faithful, as the locust plague affected only those who did not have the seal of God on their foreheads (Rev 9:4). However, the last two verses of chapter 9 indicate that John expected humanity to continue in its sinfulness.

Revelation 10—11—The Scroll, the Witnesses, and the Seventh Trumpet

Inserted within the cycle of the trumpets (chapter 10) is an interlude analogous to that of the visions inserted into the cycle of the seals. However, it does not serve as the climax to the cycle of the trumpets as the previous interlude did for the seals. As was the case with the seals, this interlude involves a twofold vision, but the two visions are not as similar to each other as the visions of the 144,000 and the multitude. These visions are of the angel with the scroll and the two witnesses. While inserted within this phase of the heavenly intervention, and as an interlude to the cycle of the trumpets, the two visions instead look ahead. They serve to anticipate the second major cycle of visions in the Book of Revelation (12:1—22:5) and provide a link between the two halves of the book.

In Revelation 4:1 John was taken up through the open door to the heavenly throne room. Now, in the first of these two visions John finds himself back on the island of Patmos and the angel comes down to him. His vision of the angel with the scroll (10:1–3) is similar to that of his initial vision of the Son of man (Rev 1:12–16). This is the second "mighty" angel described in Revelation—the first was associated with the sealed scroll (Rev 5:1–2). The angel's presence is grand and his stance with one foot on land and the other in the sea shows his size and power over the universe (Rev 10:2).

The scroll in the hand of the mighty angel is open. Some scholars say that this is a different scroll from the one of the heavenly throne, sealed by the seven seals; others maintain that it is the same scroll, now opened. This particular scroll is described as "little" and "opened," which may distinguish it from the scroll of the seven seals, which has no description other than being sealed.

When the angel speaks, his voice is accompanied by the voices of the thunders, which John is instructed not to record. In short, he is given a revelation, which at the moment he is not to relate to his listeners (Rev 10:4). The vision does not specify whether the thunderous voices, or the angel's exclamation—which sounded like the roar of a lion (Rev 10:3)—or the message of verses 6–7 are the contents of the open scroll. The clearest message of these verses is the angel's indication that with the blowing of the seventh trumpet, the plan of God announced to the prophets will finally come to pass.

Having fulfilled his first commission in the first cycle of visions, John is now commissioned a second time to prophesy. He is instructed to devour the scroll held by the angel just as Ezekiel did at his commissioning (Ezek 3:1–4). Unlike the scroll of Ezekiel, however, the scroll eaten by John, while sweet in his mouth, turns sour in his stomach. For Ezekiel, the sweetness represented the sweetness of the word of God, even though his prophecy contained messages of terrible things. The scroll of Revelation 10 is symbolic of the pleasant news of the victory of the faithful and the bitter chastisement of the world, to which John the seer must prophesy.

Chapter 11 can be divided into the following stages:

1. The measuring of the Temple (11:1–2)
2. The preaching of the two witnesses (11:3–6)
3. The war and triumph of the beast against the witnesses (11:7–10)
4. The restoration of the witnesses (11:11–13)
5. Seventh trumpet—the triumph of the Lord and his Anointed One (11:15–19)

Stage 1. The next stage of the interlude within the trumpets begins with the measuring of the Temple. Measuring is also seen in the prophetic visions of Ezekiel (40—42) and Zechariah (2:5–9), and is associated with the Restoration of the Temple. The Temple of Jerusalem was divided into four courts, the outermost of which was allowed access by the Gentiles, who could not proceed beyond that particular courtyard. The other courts, in ascending order, were those of the women, the Israelites, and the priests. John is told not to measure the court of the Gentiles, which suggests that this particular measurement signifies the preservation of the Temple from the Gentiles.

Since the Temple had already been destroyed by the time Revelation was written, it is possible that the author of Revelation was using an image that had already been used before. In addition to the prophets who used the image of measurement, John may have been using a vision that was written during the time of the Jewish uprising. Hence, the vision of the measuring of the Temple may have originated around AD 70, during the siege that led to the destruction of the Temple. When the Roman forces penetrated the walls of Jerusalem, the Jewish rebels took refuge in the Temple, from which they made their last resistance. The rebels may have believed that the Romans would be allowed to penetrate only as far as the outer court of the Gentiles and that God would intercede to keep them from penetrating farther. Historically, of course, this did not happen. The rebels were killed and the Temple was destroyed.

For the author of Revelation, the Temple is the Christian church. The church is understood in the same sense as Christ's prediction in

John 2:19—"Destroy this temple and in three days I will raise it up." It is also consistent with the theology of 1 Peter 2:5—"like living stones, let yourselves be built into a spiritual house, to be a holy priesthood to offer spiritual sacrifices acceptable to God through Jesus Christ." The measuring of the Temple in Revelation 11:1–2, therefore, signifies God's preservation of the people who make up the church.

Stage 2. The vision of the two witnesses takes in a number of elements. In Johannine theology the purpose of witnesses is to give testimony to Jesus and the gospel. There is therefore a missionary thrust to the preaching of the two witnesses. The function of these faithful witnesses is to proclaim to the world the worship of the One on the throne. From a legal standpoint, two witnesses were required for testimony to be considered authentic. Hence, the number 2 gives this legal authenticity. Through their testimony and patient endurance, people will come to hear their message.

The witnesses are described as "the two olive trees and the two lampstands that stand before the Lord of the earth" (Rev 11:4). In Zechariah 4:3 and 4:14 this image refers to Joshua the anointed priest and Zerubbabel the anointed prince. Just as the olive trees supply oil for the seven-branched lampstand in Hebrew worship (Exod 25:31–40), so the two witnesses stand before the Lord in their service to the community.

In Revelation, however, John describes the witnesses as having "authority to shut the sky, so that no rain may fall during the days of their prophesying" and "authority over the waters to turn them into blood, and to strike the earth with every kind of plague, as often as they desire" (Rev 11:6). The first power recalls the prophet Elijah, who prophesied against Baal and was antagonized by Queen Jezebel. To demonstrate that it is Yahweh, not Baal, who provides the rain, Elijah declared a drought (1 Kgs 17:1—18:45). The second power recalls Moses, who turned the waters of Egypt into blood and afflicted Egypt with the plagues (Exod 7:14—11:10). Elijah and Moses were also the two who stood with Jesus during the transfiguration (Matt 17:3; Mark 9:4; Luke 9:30). The description of the two witnesses and the powers they possess may, therefore, serve to connect them to the Law and the Prophets.

Stage 3. The death and subsequent resurrection of the two witnesses reflects that of Jesus and expresses a destiny hoped for by the author and his readers. Like the church, which experienced persecution at the hands of the Romans (the agent of evil), the two witnesses will be conquered and killed by the wild beast of the abyss. Their corpses lie in the streets of a city symbolically named "Sodom" and "Egypt" (Rev 11:7–8), the two Old Testament symbols of immorality and oppression—lack of hospitality and slavery.[15] Their corpses are observed by "members of the peoples and tribes and languages and nations" (Rev 11:9).

Stage 4. Finally, like Christ, the witnesses arise and go up to heaven as their enemies look on. The spectacle and subsequent earthquake kills seven thousand and leads others to worship God out of fear (Rev 11:11–13). This is described as the second of the three woes.

The length of Gentile occupation of the city is to be forty-two months (three-and-a-half years). The time of the preaching of the two witnesses is to be 1,260 days (or three-and-a-half years by Jewish calculation). The time for their corpses to lie on the ground is three-and-a-half days. This same pattern of time, times, and half a time ("a year, two years, and a half a year") occurs in Daniel 7:25 and 12:7. This period of Gentile occupation, ergo persecution, will seem brief in comparison to the lengthy thousand-year reign described in Revelation 20:1–3.

Stage 5. With the blowing of the **seventh trumpet** the first half of the Book of Revelation closes with the triumph of God. God and his Anointed One take possession of the world. The whole church, symbolized in the twenty-four elders, breaks forth in thanksgiving (Rev 11:16). A typical storm theophany and a vision of God's Temple in heaven accompany the victory (Rev 11:19). The view of the ark of the covenant is an especially extraordinary instance of God's self-revelation. In Jewish religion only the high priest had the privilege of entering the Holy of Holies where the ark of the covenant was housed, and even he only once a year, on the Day of Atonement. Now the glory of God is fully displayed even to ordinary people. It is a reminder of God's new covenant with every nation that follows Jesus.

This vision contains the last two recurring elements in the pattern of Revelation—judgment and salvation. The element of persecution preceded the blowing of the first trumpet with the vision of the incense and prayers rising from the altar to God during the silence (Rev 8:4). With the blowing of the seventh trumpet the judgment of the nations is complete and the salvation of the kingdom of God is established. This is the third woe pronounced by the eagle in 8:13, which accompanied the last three trumpets. Here, it is a woe for the nations of the earth that will experience God's judgment—the destruction of those who lay the earth waste (Rev 11:18).

The seventh trumpet proclaims the coming of God's reign. However, the second half of Revelation is yet to be related. As this vision is followed by the emergence of evil on the earth, the vision of the seventh trumpet may be the author's vision of the eschatological future. The events described in the hymn of the elders (Rev 11:17–18) thus foreshadow the visions that John will experience in the second half of the book—the war with the dragon, the fall of Babylon, and the thousand-year reign of the King of kings, and so forth. In any case, now that God's initiative has rescued his faithful and laid claim to the world, the forces of evil will wage war against God in the second half of the Book of Revelation.

THE COSMIC CONFLICT

Chapter 10 introduced the second half of the Book of Revelation, when the mighty angel with the little scroll gave John his second commission to prophesy. Chapter 11 briefly summarized the content coming up in the next cycle of visions. In the vision of the two witnesses we saw illustrated the destiny of those who embrace the gospel and follow the Lamb who was slain. This involves both suffering and death with the promise of resurrection. Now the beast emerges from the abyss for the first time and will be among the major figures in the second half of the book.

Each vision of the second half of Revelation tells the same story. The visions are linked as a literary device to underscore that the stories are connected. Each vision leads into the next, from which the same revelation is relayed and the same message told from different perspectives. The three major parts of Revelation

12—22 follow a pattern in which the cosmic battle between the heavenly and earthly realms is portrayed (see Fig. 12 below).

In the first part, those who worship the dragon and the two beasts are contrasted with the companions of the Lamb (Rev 12—14). In the second the seven bowls pouring forth the seven last plagues are linked to the fall of Babylon (Rev 16—19:10). Finally, the great millennium of the King of kings is linked to the vision of the new creation (Rev 19:11—22:5). While part 1 contains a contrast within itself, part 2 as a whole is contrasted with part 3; the wrath against the kings of earth is contrasted with the reign of the King of kings encompassed in the new creation, the image of Babylon (the harlot) with the image of the New Jerusalem (the bride).

Here again, we see the pattern of persecution, judgment, and salvation. In the vision of the anti-Trinity we see persecution (Rev 12—13). Judgment comes in the harvest of the earth (Rev 14:14–20). A brief account of salvation follows the harvest in Revelation 15:2–4, prior to the pouring forth of the seven last plagues. In addition, the next three cycles of visions as a whole contain this pattern on a grander scale. The cycle of the beast and the companions of the Lamb contain heavy elements of persecution (Rev 12—14). The cycle of the seven last plagues (Rev 15—18) contains God's

Figure 12

REVELATION 12—22

PART 1:12-14	Anti-Trinity ⟷ Companions of the Lamb	*persecution*
14:14-20	Harvest of the Earth	*judgment*
15:2-4	Song of the Victors	*salvation*
PART 2: 15:5—19:10	Seven Last Plagues/Fall of Babylon	*judgment*
PART 3: 19:11—22:5	Victory of the King of Kings/New Creation	*salvation*

(⟷ = Contrasting Images)

judgment upon Babylon. Finally, the cycle of the great millennium and the new creation contains the dominant theme of salvation.

The second half of Revelation returns the reader to the principal theme found at the beginning of the first half—Jesus as Messiah. Just as the first cycle of visions began with the vision of the Lamb receiving worship on the heavenly throne, the second cycle ends with Jesus on the throne, receiving the same worship. Hence, Revelation as a whole begins and ends with the principal message of the book: the victory of Christ. Jesus is the frame that binds the revelation. He alone receives authentic worship and protects those who believe in him. He alone wins the victory over Satan and the powers of evil. The single revelation put forth by the visions of John is that Jesus Christ is the focus of our faith and the source of our salvation.

Revelation 12—13—The Anti-Trinity

The image of and conflict between the woman and the dragon are drawn from a number of sources and contain both combat and mythic elements. Some of the imagery is taken from the Old Testament. The dreams of Jacob's son Joseph include a vision of the stars. In the dream the eleven stars representing Joseph's brothers bow down before Joseph (Gen 37:9). In addition, much pagan imagery from this period, particularly those drawn from Babylonian mythology, include images of goddesses crowned with twelve stars, the twelve principal signs of the astrological zodiac. We have already seen how the twenty-four elders may have been drawn from the twelve stars of the north and twelve of the south, which represent the twenty-four gods of Babylonian astronomy and, therefore, the cosmos. We also recognize the occurrence of twelve as symbolizing either the twelve tribes of Israel, or the twelve apostles, or both. Now the woman giving birth takes on the persona of a figure clothed with the cosmos.

The story of the woman and the dragon is a typical archetype in ancient mythology in which a cosmic battle results from the emergence of a beast that threatens the cosmic order. A young hero is destined to destroy the beast and restore order. The beast seeks to prevent the hero's rise to power by attacking either his mother or the hero himself when he is a helpless infant. Many stories in both the ancient cultures as well as in modern storytelling reflect this archetype. The Greek hero Heracles is one example in which the goddess Hera attempts to kill the infant Heracles with two serpents. Anyone familiar with the 1984 movie *The Terminator* will recognize this pattern in the story about a robot assassin from the future pursuing a woman who will eventually give birth to a son destined to overthrow a future robotic oppression of humans. Even the story of Christ contains this archetype: in Matthew's Gospel, King Herod slaughters the innocents in an attempt to destroy the infant Jesus, whom Herod regards as a threat to his kingly power.

The Greek story of the sun god Apollo, Leto his mother, and Python bears the closest similarity to that of the woman and the dragon:[16] Python, the dragon that guarded the oracle of Delphi, had learned by prophecy that a child of Leto would replace him as the ruler of the oracle. When the monster learned that Leto was pregnant, he pursued her over the known earth in an effort to prevent her from giving birth. Leto attempted escape by taking the form of an eagle, but Python prevented her from landing so as to give birth. Zeus, however, allowed Leto to take refuge with his brother Poseidon, lord of the sea, who hid her on the island of Delos, which floated without foundation on the surface of the sea. Poseidon allowed the sea to swallow the island, thereby hiding Leto from Python. Unable to find her, Python returned to Delphi. Substitute the woman for Leto, the child for Apollo, and the dragon for Python, and you have the apocalyptic image of the woman and the dragon.

It is possible that the author of Revelation incorporated classical images, which were familiar to the people of the late first century, into the literary expressions of early Christian theology (see Fig. 13 on the next page). The dragon is a threat to the cosmos in that its tail "swept down a third of the stars of heaven and threw them to the earth" (Rev 12:4). The son born of the woman, however, is destined to shepherd all the nations, bringing order amid the threat of chaos. Hence, the dragon seeks to destroy the child when it is born. Instead the child is taken up to God's throne while the woman takes refuge in the desert, where the earth protects her by swallowing the flood that comes forth from the dragon's mouth.

Figure 13

REVELATION 12: SOURCE AND SYMBOLISM				
Mythology	*Imagery*	*Genesis*	*Salvation History*	*Ecclesiology*
Leto	**Woman**	Eve	Heavenly Israel	Mother Church
Apollo	**Child**	Offspring	Messiah	Christians
Python	**Dragon**	Serpent	Satan	Satan/Persecutions

Unable to capture either the woman or her child, the dragon turns on "the rest of [the woman's] children, those who keep God's commandments and hold the testimony of Jesus" (Rev 12:5–6, 13–17).

A number of interpretations have been proposed for this story. Some scholars see a cosmic parallel to the conflict between Eve and the serpent in the Garden of Eden (Gen 3:15). Others claim that the woman personifies the heavenly Israel, the spouse of God by covenant,[17] from whom was born the Messiah, a child of Israel. In another interpretation, however, Old Israel is giving birth to the New Israel, the church. Satan, through the persecution by Rome, seeks to destroy the offspring of Old Israel while it is still in infancy. Still others propose that the woman represents Holy Mother Church, whose offspring, Christians, are threatened by the power of Satan, who seeks to destroy through Roman persecution those who follow Christ.

Perhaps the most notable interpretation that has come out of church tradition is that the woman represents Mary, the mother of Jesus. The connection to Mary, however, did not come until the fourth century, when Marian devotion began to flourish in the church. The woman is described in such superhuman terms that the author may not have intended to identify her with a single human being. However, since we honor Mary as the "New Eve" and "Image and Mother of the church," a Marian interpretation can be reconciled to the image of the woman in that both Mary and the woman symbolize the same thing. Therefore, this passage from Revelation is read on the Solemnity of the Assumption, and is offered as an optional reading for Marian feasts during the Easter season. It is unlikely, however, that the author of Revelation intended Mary as the focus of this image.

The war that breaks out in heaven is the traditional story of Satan's rebellion against God, in which Satan is vanquished by Michael and expelled from the heavenly realm. In the hymn that follows (Rev 12:10–12) Satan is referred to as the "accuser." This may stem from the character of Satan as presented in Job 1—2. Satan is a member of the court of heaven who serves as an accuser or prosecutor, a "devil's advocate" who tests the true fidelity of God's faithful. His role is not so much that of an evil one or the devil as that of an adversary, who spies on the wrongdoing of humanity and reports it to his master, who is God. In the Book of Revelation, Satan's identity is extended to be the personification of evil and the one who seduces humanity away from the worship of God. He is still seen as the accuser (Rev 12:10) and it is as accuser that he is cast out of heaven.

The vision of the **first beast** (Rev 13), which follows that of the woman and the dragon, symbolizes the Roman Empire by combining all of the elements of the four beasts in Daniel's vision, which symbolize the world empires. While Daniel 7 describes the fourth beast in vague terms, Revelation 13 describes the first beast more clearly. The combination of the bear-like paws, the mouth of a lion, and the appearance of a leopard signifies that Rome is equal to or worse than the combined powers of the four empires symbolically described in Daniel. The blasphemous activity of the beast (Rev 13:5–6) reflects another vision of Daniel, that of the ram and the he-goat (Dan 8) in which the little horn speaks arrogant blasphemies against God.

The seven heads are later described as representing the Seven Hills of Rome as well as the seven kings (emperors) who had reigned up to that point—Augustus, Tiberius, Caligula, Claudius, Nero, Vespasian, and Titus (Rev 17:9). While a handful of emperors existed between some of these named (such as the three who reigned between Nero and Vespasian), these seven were the principal emperors up to that point whose reigns were marked by stability in the emperor's power. As the number 7 indicates totality, the heads could represent all Roman emperors. The blasphemous names would represent the title of "god," which the emperors took to themselves so as to assume and promote the image and cult of their divinity.

The first beast is presented as a distorted parallel to the Lamb—an anti-Son or anti-Christ image. First, it receives power from the dragon, as well as its throne and its great authority (Rev 13:2), just as the Lamb received worship that had been extended to him from the One on the throne (Rev 5:7ff.). Second, the first beast appears to have been slain when in fact it has not. Unlike the Lamb who had been slain, the wound on the beast only appears to be mortal, when in fact it is described as healed. Hence, the first beast is a deceiver. This image of one of the seven heads appearing to have a mortal wound, which in reality was healed, may represent a growing legend of the period that Nero would come back to life. This legend coincides with the early Christian idea of an anti-Christ and would have been an opposing expectation to the return of Christ—the Lamb who was slain. The letters of John give an example of early Christian awareness of the anti-Christ: a deceiver who denies that Jesus is the Christ (1 John 2:22; 4:3; 2 John 1:7). The anti-Christ or beast of Revelation demands worship for itself, to lure people away from the true worship of Christ. Such a figure is seen in the Roman emperor, who demanded worship as part of Roman religion.

The **second beast** is a parody of the seven spirits before God (or the Holy Spirit) described in 1:4 and 5:6. It is described in terms of false prophecy; its power "makes the earth and its inhabitants worship the first beast" (Rev 13:12). It also has the power to give life to the beast's image "so that the image of the beast could even speak and cause those who would not worship the image of the beast to be killed" (Rev 13:15). Just as the Holy Spirit is the inspiration behind our faith and worship of Christ, so too is the second beast to the false worship of the first beast. Thus the dragon and the two beasts make up an anti-Trinity, meant to be an inverted parody to the goodness of the Holy Trinity.

On the political level, the second beast may represent the local Roman authority of Asia Minor. Like the second beast, Roman politicians would act with the authority of the emperor and even promote the worship of the emperor so as to advance their own political stature. In the same way, the priests of the Roman cult would be symbolized in the second beast insofar as they give meaning and "life" to the cult of the emperor. The priests of the Roman religion would also fit more closely the image of a false prophet that the second beast exemplifies.

Finally, the second beast forces all people of all social classes to be marked on their right hands or their foreheads (Rev 13:16). This too can be seen as a parody of the seal of God that marks the foreheads of the servants of God. The mark of the beast can also be compared to that of slaves of this period who were branded with the mark of their owner, or to devout soldiers who branded themselves with the name of their general. The prohibition of Revelation 13:17 may be taken from a social practice in which those who did not carry some seal, mark, or indication of loyalty or devotion to the emperor were not granted service or business in the market-place, a kind of anti-Christian apartheid in Roman society. Also, when a man had burned incense to the emperor he was given a certificate verifying that he had done so, certifying his act of worship.[18] For a Christian to obtain one would mean that the Christian had denied his or her faith. In the context of Revelation, the mark of the beast may parallel any or all of these practices. In any case, it signifies one's acceptance of the beast's authority, one's devotion to the beast, or that the beast owns the one who is marked, as a slave is owned by its master.

Chapter 13 concludes with what is one of the most extensively interpreted verses in the Scriptures, the number of the beast (Rev 13:18). The number 666 has come to represent the very essence of evil. But who is the beast that is so numbered? In ancient societies, including Jewish, Greek, and Roman, the alphabet carried a numerical value in each letter, in addition to serving as a system of reading and writing. It would be as if we, in English, were to use such numeric values as 1 for the letter *A*, 2 for *B*, 3 for *C*, or any numeric value for each letter of our alphabet, regardless of order. When letters were combined into words, the word as a whole took on a numeric value that was the sum total of the letters. Most scholars, therefore, identify the number of the beast as being the numerical value of Nero, the notorious emperor whose name has become synonymous with anti-Christian persecution. While various calculations have been put forth, the most commonly accepted interpretation among scholars is that the Greek form of the name "Caesar Nero" *(Neron Caesar)* comes to 666 (the letter *N* equaling the number 50).[19] This interpretation coincides with other Roman-Nero imagery in Revelation.

In a broader interpretation, the number 6, being one less than 7 (perfection), would also represent imperfection. Since stating a quality three times gave it emphasis ("Holy, holy, holy"—Isa 6:3; Rev 4:8), 666 would signify the epitome of imperfection. Some scholars contrast this with Revelation 19:16, in which the numerical value of "King of kings" and "Lord of lords" is 777 (epitome of perfection).[20]

Revelation 14—The Companions of the Lamb and the Harvest of the Earth

The anti-Trinity and the followers of the beast are contrasted with the image of the Lamb and his followers—a reappearance of the 144,000 originally seen in Revelation 7:1–8. The Lamb stands as a contrast to the beast. Mount Zion, the presence of God and the realm of cosmic order, is a contrast to the sea, the abyss of chaos and destruction. Finally, the 144,000 who are sealed with the Lamb's name and the name of his Father stand as a contrast to the followers of the beast, who are sealed with his stamped image. They also contrast with the fallen angels who with the dragon were driven from the heavenly realm. Just as those angels fell to earth, the companions of the Lamb rise to heaven.

They are without blemish or flaw, thus calling to mind the vision of the martyrs beneath the heavenly altar and foreshadowing those in Revelation 20:4, who are described as having been "beheaded for their testimony to Jesus and for the word of God. They had not worshiped the beast or its image and had not received its mark on their foreheads or their hands."

In 1 Enoch the fallen angels are described as having engaged in illicit sexual intercourse.[21] In this way another contrast can be drawn between fallen angels and the companions of the Lamb, whose sexual purity is described in Revelation 14:4—"It is these who have not defiled themselves with women, for they are virgins; these follow the Lamb wherever he goes." The language of sexual purity can also be contrasted with the previous image of the harlot Jezebel, or the following image of the whore of Babylon, both of whom sell themselves to the lewdness of idolatry. Hence, these 144,000 are described as chaste and virginal because they followed the Lamb and did not yield to idolatry.

Certain details in Revelation 14:1–5 suggest that the companions represent a special group and not simply all of the faithful (as may have been true of the 144,000 in Revelation 7:4, 9). First, they sing a new hymn to the Lord. Unlike the song of the four living creatures and the elders quoted in Revelation 5:9f., the new song sung by the companions is not quoted. The reader is not told what the words of this new song are, which indicates further a sense of exclusivity. They do not simply follow the Lamb, but accompany him wherever he goes. They are described as "redeemed from humankind as first fruits for God and the Lamb" (Rev 14:4). "First fruits" suggest they are of a sacrificial quality.

The three angels declare three things. A declaration of joy is followed by a woe and finally a warning. The first angel issues a call to conversion and a call to worship God (Rev 14:6–7). In a pagan culture in which gods and goddesses are linked to the various elements of the cosmos, the call of the angels declares God "him who made heaven and earth, the sea and the springs of water," thereby placing God as master of the cosmic order.

The second angel declares that Babylon has fallen (Rev 14:8). Here the author borrows from Isaiah 21:9 and Jeremiah 51:8. In Revelation, however, Babylon represents Rome, the New Babylon and the second pagan power to destroy Jerusalem and the Temple. Here again Babylonian idolatry is spoken of in terms of lewdness and harlotry. The "wine of her fornication" contrasts with the "wine of God's wrath" found in Revelation 14:10, warns against worshiping the beast, and anticipates the lengthier declaration of Babylon's fall in Revelation 18. The third angel issues a final warning, intended as a further incentive for the reader to remain faithful to Jesus and the commandments of God (Rev 14:9–12).

The three angels are followed by a voice from heaven that declares the second of the seven beatitudes of the Book of Revelation (Rev 14:13)—"blessed are the dead who from now on die in the Lord...they will rest from their labors, for their deeds follow them." The threats are balanced by the beatitude's suggestion of reward, which is not specifically limited to those who have been beheaded for their witness to Christ. The last sentence of this verse has inspired one of the prayers in the Rite of Christian Burial, so that Catholic liturgy extends this beatitude to all those who die with Christ in baptism and eventually die believing in him.

Chapter 14 concludes with the harvest of the earth, a vision that draws on prophetic imagery. The image of "one like a son of man" recalls again the angelic image of Daniel 7:13. Like Daniel, the author of Revelation does not use the term as a title, but rather as a description—like *a* son of man, not *the* Son of man. Unlike the individual of Revelation 1:13–16 this individual is not specifically identified, nor does his description suggest any specific individual. Hence we cannot state emphatically that the figure is Christ.

The taking of the sickle to the harvest is drawn from Joel 4:13,[22] in which the images of harvest and winepress symbolize a holy war between the divine and the nations that have done violence to the Jews. In Revelation the image refers to divine judgment upon the earth. This image of the winepress as a symbol of the wrath of God will be seen again in the battle between Christ and the beast in 19:15. Since 19:15 clearly states that it is Christ who will tread out the winepress, it can be concluded that the one like a son of man in 14:14 is an angelic being who wields the sickle.

The vision of the harvest is an image of great violence, as the one like a son of man, along with another angel, reaps the harvest of the earth and gathers the "grapes" into the huge "wine press of the wrath of God" (Rev 14:19). The judgment is compared to the trampling of grapes and the bloodshed described as covering the land for two hundred miles, rising as high as a horse's bridle (Rev 14:19–20). The battle, however, is only hinted at. Like the declaration of Revelation 14:8, the battle of the harvest is spelled out in greater detail in the visions that follow (Rev 19:19–21).

THE FALL OF ROME

Revelation 15 is a transition chapter that links the vision of chapters 12—14 with the next series of visions. It begins with an image of salvation, which follows upon the images of persecution in Revelation 12 and 13 and judgment in 14:14–20. Revelation 15:2–4 speaks of those who had won the victory standing on a sea of glass and singing praises to God in a song reminiscent of Moses' song following the Exodus from Egypt. The crowd calls to mind the multitude of Revelation 7:9, and the sea of glass recalls the sea of glass in the heavenly realm (Rev 4:6).

The chapter begins and ends with preparation for the seven final plagues that will deliver the wrath of God (Rev 15:1, 5–8). The tent of witness is the name of the tent as described in the Greek text of Exodus 40. Here final preparation is made for God to exercise judgment on the wicked, ultimately encompassed in Babylon, the symbol of Rome.

Revelation 16—The Seven Bowls

The final plagues echo once again the cycle of the seals and the trumpets. Seven bowls are to be poured forth to bring about God's wrath. With the seals, social justice and vindication accompany God's wrath in the form of the four horsemen, who bring social upheaval, and the martyrs, who cry for justice against their oppressors. With the trumpets, God's wrath predominantly affects the natural elements and the cosmic order. The seven bowls bring forth God's wrath from a different perspective (see Fig. 14 below).

The dominant theme is judgment upon the beast and its followers. This is politicized by the inclusion of Babylon as a recipient of judgment. Just as the beast was foreshadowed in Revelation 11:7 before being more fully described in Revelation 13, so too the harlot Babylon is hinted at 16:19—following the seventh bowl—before being described in greater detail in Revelation 17. The fall

Figure 14

THE SEVEN BOWLS AND THE SEVEN LAST PLAGUES
Bowl 1 Boils (*affecting only sinners*)
Bowl 2 Sea turned to *blood*
Bowl 3 Rivers and springs turned to *blood*
Bowl 4 Men burned with *fire*—God's name blasphemed
Bowl 5 Kingdom plunged into *darkness*—God's name blasphemed
Bowl 6 Euphrates dried up—kings of the earth gather at *Armageddon*
Bowl 7 *Storm theophany*—earthquake/hailstones—God blasphemed

of Babylon is likewise hinted at in 14:8 before its description in Revelation 18.

With a few exceptions, the principal plagues of Egypt are applied to the judgment of God's wrath in the Book of Revelation. In the cycles of the trumpets and bowls six of the ten plagues that fell upon Egypt (Exod 7:14—11:10) fall upon the earth.

1. Water turned to blood (Exod 7:19–24)—Rev 8:8, 10–11; 16:3–4
2. Frogs (Exod 7:25—8:10)—Rev 16:13
3. Gnats (Exod 8:12–15)
4. Flies (Exod 8:16–20)
5. Pestilence (Exod 9:3–6)
6. Boils (Exod 9:8–11)—Rev 16:2
7. Hail (Exod 9:13–26)—Rev 8:7; 16:21
8. Locusts (Exod 10:12–19)—Rev 9:3–11
9. Darkness (Exod 10:21–23)—Rev 8:12; 16:10
10. Death of the firstborn (Exod 11:4–8; 12:29–30)

The seven bowls further increase the intensity of God's wrath. Whereas the seals affected one-fourth of the earth and the trumpets affected one-third, the wrath of the bowls is not limited. The bowls are poured out onto the earth, the sea, and the rivers with no specific percentage named, which thus implies yet another increase in the severity with which God's wrath comes upon the earth. Unlike the seals and trumpets all seven bowls are poured forth in rapid succession.

When the **first bowl** is poured (Rev 16:2) severe boils break out on those who accepted the mark of the beast and worshiped its image. The plague, therefore, affects only sinners guilty of idolatry— those who give worship to the Roman emperor rather than to Christ. This plague recalls the plague of boils unleashed on Egypt during the Exodus (Exod 9:8–12). The **second** and **third bowls** again recall the first plague on Egypt as the sea and rivers turn to blood, killing every living creature within them (Rev 16:3). The hymn given by the angel (Rev 16:5–6) and the altar (Rev 16:7) further affirm God's justice despite persecutions and other circumstances that appear to imply the opposite. As the heavenly altar also had an angel the words of the altar can be interpreted as the voice of that angel responding to the angel of verse 5.

The **fourth bowl** causes the sun to burn with fire—thus indicating an intensifying of the sun's heat—while the **fifth bowl** plunges the kingdom into darkness (Rev 16:8–10), which implies a blocking or extinguishing of the sun's light, thereby causing severe darkness. Whereas the fourth bowl involves a plague issuing forth from the cosmic order, the fifth bowl offers a historical setting to the plagues in that the "throne of the beast" is that of the Roman emperor, who received his power and authority from the dragon (Satan). It is this kingdom that is plunged into darkness, which again evokes memories of the ninth plague upon Egypt (Exod 10:22–23a; Rev 8:12). The fourth and fifth bowls also include a notation that those who were affected had blasphemed the name of God (Rev 16:9, 11). Despite their knowledge of God and their suffering during the divine judgment, the blasphemers fail to repent and continue in their wickedness.

The **sixth bowl** refers to the river Euphrates. The river dries up to prepare for the gathering of the kings of the east (Rev 16:12). This links the sixth bowl and its plague to the sixth trumpet, from which issued the symbolic invasion of the Parthians suggested by the four angels who were bound at the Euphrates. Like the blowing of the sixth trumpet, the sixth bowl heralds the preparation for a great battle.

Demonic imagery is combined with military imagery, and demonic influence is attributed to the gathering of the earthly forces. The dragon, the beast, and the "false prophet"—the second beast—assemble the kings of the earth for the final battle. The frog-like spirits that issue forth from the mouths of the dragon and the two beasts (Rev 16:13–14) call to mind yet another plague upon Egypt (Exod 8:1–3). Frogs were considered unclean animals (Lev 11:10) and therefore represented the uncleanness of the summons issued to the kings who gather around the dragon and the beasts.

In the midst of the gathering (Rev 16:15) John briefly inserts a traditional prophetic utterance (Matt 24:43–44; Luke 12:39–40; 1 Thess 5:2, 4; 2 Pet 3:10), which may have been intended to connect the gathering of the kings with the coming of the Christ. This gathering is also linked to the battle that will be described in

Revelation 19:11–21, the victory of the King of kings. This battle precedes the thousand-year reign and the Last Judgment (Rev 20), thus further associating the great battle with Christ's return in glory. The third beatitude of the Book of Revelation is a part of this insert.

Finally, the plague of the **seventh bowl** is described with the motifs of traditional storm theophany (Rev 16:17–21). This theophany, however, has intensity unlike any before—it is a theophany to end all theophanies. The inclusion of giant hailstones calls to mind yet another plague that fell upon Egypt and another link to the seven trumpets (Exod 9:23b; Rev 8:7). This theophany is described in political terms as Babylon is now included in the divine wrath of the seven last plagues (Rev 16:19). The inclusion of Babylon serves as a coda to the seven last plagues as well as a link to the next vision, which depicts in greater detail Babylon's corruption and fall.

Revelation 16:16—Armageddon

The word *Armageddon* has become synonymous with worldwide crisis, war, and destruction. It has been closely associated with the end times because the Book of Revelation describes it as being the climax of God's judgment, preceding the return of Christ. To the people of the first century AD, however, Armageddon (a Hebrew name) had special meaning.

If the Book of Revelation were written today, the name of the location might read: "The devils then assembled the kings in a place called in English 'Gettysburg.'" Other names could easily be substituted: Normandy, Antietam, Bastogne, the Bulge, or Stalingrad. These places in recent history have come to be closely associated with war, where epic battles and tremendous bloodshed occurred. If the site chosen were Waterloo, then the site would also be associated with decisive defeat, in this case Napoleon's. The same is true for Armageddon to the people of ancient Israel and early Christianity. Armageddon is not an event or a catastrophe. Armageddon, as stated in Revelation, is a place or location of a great battle.

Armageddon, or *har-megiddo*, is most commonly identified as the Mountain of Megiddo, overlooking the plain of Jezreel, on

Ivory decoration from a Canaanite palace at Megiddo showing the victorious army bringing prisoners and booty before the king on his throne decorated with cherubim.

which the ancient city, Megiddo, was built. To the people of ancient Palestine and early Christianity Megiddo was the location of great battles and much bloodshed. One of the features of the Promised Land, the Palestinian region, is that it was right in the middle of four empires—Egypt, Assyria, Babylon, and Persia; Greece and Rome would come later. Hence, throughout the history of Israel, military enemies menaced the people and threatened the security of the nation. Megiddo was the site of a major crossroad between these empires. Whoever controlled Megiddo had great influence over the trade and commerce of the region. In fact, from the time of ancient Israel up to World War I, Megiddo was one of the great battlegrounds of the Middle East, and Mount Megiddo would have been a prime location for military leaders because of the vista it provided over the vast plain of Jezreel. Therefore, the people thought of Megiddo the same way we think of Gettysburg, Normandy, and other cities where great battles took place.

This site is mentioned a number of times in the Bible, some of which are associated with decisive battles or military buildup. To name a few:

> The kings came, they fought; then fought the kings of Canaan, at Taanach, by the waters of Megiddo. (Judg 5:19)

> King Josiah went to meet him; but when Pharaoh Neco met him at Megiddo, he killed him. (2 Kgs 23:29; cf. also 2 Chr 35:22)

> On that day the mourning in Jerusalem will be as great as the mourning for Hadad-rimmon in the plain of Megiddo. (Zech 12:11)

While a plain is a much more likely battleground than a mountain, the use of Armageddon is less about geography and more of a symbolic location to emphasize further the magnitude of the final decisive battle between the Lamb and the forces of evil.

A certain irony, however, should be noted in Revelation's use of Armageddon as a symbolic location. In previous calls for war (the first four seals and the sixth trumpet) the call comes from heaven and war occurs (four riders, four angels). The irony of the sixth bowl and the gathering at Armageddon is that it is the realm of evil—in that of the dragon and the beasts—that calls for war (Rev 16:13–16), but war does not occur (see Fig. 15 below).

In the more detailed description of the battle of Armageddon (Rev 19:11–21) the gathering of forces builds up to a point in Revelation 19:19. However, no battle takes place. Rather, the beasts are overwhelmed by the power of the King of kings and victory is declared without battle! Therefore, where Revelation is concerned, the name *Armageddon* no longer means war, but victory. In the overall theology of Revelation, the victory of Christ is in his death and resurrection—a victory that cannot be undone, even by persecution of his church.

Revelation 17:1—19:10—The Fall of Babylon

The vision of the fall of Babylon depicts the final fall of the Roman Empire. The vision of Revelation 14:8 and 16:19 is spelled out in more detail in 17:1—19:10. We see for the first time the infamous whore of Babylon riding the scarlet beast. The beast has seven heads and ten horns and is covered with blasphemous names. Described as richly dressed and adorned in wealth that recalls the

Figure 15

IRONY OF ARMAGEDDON			
Seals 1–4	*Four horsemen*	*Heaven* calls for war	War comes
Sixth trumpet	*Four angels*	*Heaven* calls for war	War comes
Sixth bowl	*Gathering at Armageddon*	*Evil* calls for war	War *does not* come

wealth of Rome, the whore is identified as Babylon, the mother of harlots and abominations, drunk with the blood of the martyrs (Rev 17:3–6). The fact that her identification is written on her forehead echoes those who have the mark of the Lamb and the beast on their foreheads. This was also a common form of identification for Roman prostitutes. The verses that follow describe the meaning of these images.

The beast that the harlot rides "was and is not and is to come" (Rev 17:8), a negative distortion of the One who is, who was, and who is to come, and of Christ, who lived, died, and will come again. The seven heads are seven hills, the traditional reference to the city of Rome. They also represent seven kings, five of whom have fallen, one of whom is presently reigning, and another who is to come (Rev 17:9). As previously mentioned, these kings may represent the seven earlier Roman emperors whose reigns were marked by stability in their power. However, there is little agreement as to their identity.

The ten horns are ten more kings not yet crowned. Some scholars suggest that this alludes again to the Parthians on the eastern frontier of the empire. In the vision of John the ten horns of the beast turn against the harlot, strip her of her riches, devour her flesh, and set her afire (Rev 17:16–17). It is a prophecy of the doom of Rome that makes use of the legend that the emperor Nero would return. When Nero saw that he could no longer remain in power, he considered fleeing to Parthia before finally taking his own life. Legend grew that he had not died, and it was believed that ten satraps of Parthia would accompany the revived Nero in his march on Rome to regain power. John incorporated and adapted this legend to fit his apocalyptic scheme, that the powers of the beast (Nero, or the emperor) will betray its instrument (the whore, Rome), in order to solidify its authority prior to the great battle against God.

This is done in accord with God's plan and shows that God never loses control of human affairs. God destroys Rome (encompassed in Babylon) by means of the beast. God uses apparent misfortune and persecution as part of the divine plan to work out the ultimate triumph over evil (see Rev 6:11).

Following the description of the whore of Babylon and her destruction at the hands of the beast, Revelation 18 presents a series of laments over Babylon's fall that follow upon the themes of Babylon's condemnation and destruction spoken of in the previous chapter. A chorus of joy over the wedding of the Lamb counters this lament in 19:1–10.

Unlike the rest of the Book of Revelation, Babylon's fall, which prophesies the fall of Rome, is not witnessed firsthand. The series of dirges or "doom songs" portray the reaction to the fall in a series of six scenes in which different groups lament the fall. In the first scene an angel comes down from heaven with great authority (Rev 18:1–3). This is followed by another voice from heaven (Rev 18:4–8). The third scene involves the lament by the kings of the earth who committed fornication with Babylon (Rev 18:9–10) and is followed by the merchants of the world. The fourth and fifth scenes consist of two songs, one by the merchants (Rev 18:11–17a) and the other by the captains, navigators, sailors, and seafaring men (Rev 18:17b–19). Finally, the chapter concludes with a declaration by another angel (Rev 18:21–24). Inserted within this series of dirges is a call for rejoicing in 18:20.

The laments follow the tradition and literature of the Hebrew prophets who sang dirges over Babylon and other Hebrew enemies. Chief among them are Isaiah and Jeremiah. Isaiah prophesied against Babylon in 13:19–22, 21:1–10, and 47:1-15,[23] and against Edom in 34:11–15. Jeremiah gives two prophecies against Babylon (chapters 50—51) in light of the Jewish Exile. (See Fig. 16 below for two examples of their use in Revelation.)

The lament of the merchants shares features with Ezekiel 26—27. Ironically, the merchants mourn not the loss of Babylon herself, but the loss of their markets. The products listed are items of

Figure 16

EXAMPLES OF PROPHETIC REFERENCES IN REVELATION 18	
"I shall not sit as a widow."—Isa 47:8	*"I am no widow."*—Rev 18:7
"Then the heavens and the earth, and all that is in them, shall shout for joy over Babylon."—Jer 51:48	*"Rejoice over her, O heaven."* —Rev 18:20

great luxury (Rev 12—13), which implies a tension between wealth and the Christian message. Hence the merchants lament out of greed, since the markets from which they drew their wealth are now gone.

The kings, merchants, and sea captains all observe the punishment of Babylon from a distance. Similar to the beast, which turned against Babylon, the kings who shared in her power and corruption and the merchants who grew wealthy from dealing with Babylon now abandon her. They "will stand far off, in fear of her torment" (Rev 18:15). While this echoes the disciples of Christ, who fearfully kept their distance when he was crucified (Luke 23:49), it really depicts the agent of evil being abandoned by those who sought to profit from dealing with her.

The image of the angel casting a stone into the sea echoes Jeremiah 51:63–64, in which Jeremiah casts a stone into the Euphrates, declaring that the river will swallow up Babylon. Since Babylon rested along the Euphrates, Jeremiah declares that it will sink into the river. In the context of Revelation, the stone is cast into the sea symbolizing that Rome, the New Babylon, will be cast, not into the river, but into the sea beside which it rests.

A chorus of joy in Revelation 19:1–10 follows the lament over Babylon. While different from the laments of chapter 18, the chorus is linked to the laments by Revelation 18:20, a call to rejoice. Revelation 19:1–8 is the response to that call. In the songs of rejoicing we hear of the marriage of the Lamb to his bride (Rev 19:7–9). The bride who marries the Lamb contrasts sharply with the whore that "rides" the beast.

The theme of the marriage of God with God's people is found in the Old Testament. For example, the Song of Songs reflects God's love for his bride Israel, with whom he shares a covenant. As part of his witness to an unfaithful Israel, the prophet Hosea is commanded to marry an unfaithful wife. How he deals with her reflects God and his relationship with God's people (Hos 2:16–22). In the New Testament, marriage imagery is applied to the covenant between Christ and his church. St. Paul writes that the church is "betrothed…to one husband" presented "as a chaste virgin to Christ" (2 Cor 11:2). The fourth beatitude of the Book of Revelation states: "Blessed are those who are invited to the marriage supper of the Lamb" (Rev 19:9). The bride of the Lamb is described as dressed in finest white linen, which symbolizes the good deeds of the saints (Rev 19:8). For early Christians this further emphasizes the necessity of good deeds (see Rev 14:12).

Revelation 19:1–10 is the only passage in the New Testament in which the common religious praise "Alleluia" appears, uttered four times. With the exception of various psalms that have the word as part of their titles,[24] it is the only place in the entire Bible where "Alleluia" appears as part of the text. The assembly in heaven utters the first chorus (Rev 19:1–2), with the third "alleluia" proclaimed by the twenty-four elders and the four living creatures. The second chorus is a song of victory sung by what sounds like "a great multitude, like the sound of many waters and like the sound of mighty thunderpeals" (Rev 19:6–8) and is called for by the voice coming from the throne (Rev 19:6).

In Revelation 19:10 John falls down to worship the angel who has shown him this vision. He is reprimanded, ordered to get up, and told that worship belongs to God alone. This episode is repeated almost verbatim in Revelation 22:8b–9. John's falling down to worship is consistent with the Jewish belief that angels manifested God's glory and also served as intermediaries. The reader, with John, is now reminded that with the coming of Jesus, angelic intermediaries between God and humanity are no longer necessary.

THE FINAL VICTORY AND THE NEW CREATION

We reach the climax of the Book of Revelation, in which the conquering King of kings at last makes his appearance. Here the Book of Revelation depicts Jesus in his second coming. The theme of the warrior Messiah echoes the ancient Canaanite and Hebrew image of the warrior god, who comes forth to conquer Satan and bring salvation to those who believe in him. Eventually Jesus will be identified as the Lamb who sits on the throne, and it will be he who ushers in the new creation and the New Jerusalem in which he and the Lord God Almighty serve as the Temple.

The themes of persecution, judgment, and salvation recur as Satan is unleashed and attacks the beloved city of God's people

(Rev 20:7–9a). Satan is quickly vanquished (vv. 9b–10) and the rest of the book describes the events of salvation in detail. This brings an overall balance to the second half of the Book of Revelation, which began with the persecution of the dragon and the beasts as the predominant theme (Rev 12–14), included the harvest of the earth, and led into the seven last plagues where God's judgment prevailed. In the concluding section, which contains the final seven visions of Revelation, the theme of salvation is predominant, bringing the vision of Revelation to a close with the victory and salvation of Christ.

Revelation 19:11–21—The Victory of the King of Kings

As foretold in Revelation 17:12–18, the harlot Babylon, the symbol of Rome, must be overthrown before the dragon and the beasts are vanquished. Having sung the victory hymn over the fall of Babylon and celebrated the wedding feast of the Lamb, the heavenly realm turns to the final battle against the forces of the dragon and the beasts (Rev 19:1–10).

Scholars have identified this episode as a more detailed depiction of the battle of Armageddon foreshadowed in Revelation 16:16. A great battle never takes place, however. The King of kings and Lord of lords makes his dramatic appearance with his armies of heaven. A feast is then declared. The scene reaches a climax with the vision of the beast and the kings of the earth mustering to make war on the King of kings (19:19). However, the enemies of the King of kings are not described as even putting up a fight. Rather, in the verses immediately following, the beast is captured along with the false prophet (the second beast). Both are hurled into the fiery pool of sulphur while the rest of the dragon's armies are slain (Rev 19:21). The only one left is the dragon.

The opening of the heavens is a typical apocalyptic formula. The King of kings makes his appearance riding a white horse, the typical symbol of the conqueror. His eyes not only see with perfection, as is the case with the Lamb (seven eyes), but they have a judgment that is superior to that of Satan and the beasts. This is shown in the blazing of the eyes. The use of the word *diadem* refers to a crown, and the many diadems of the King of kings surpass the seven diadems on the heads of the dragon (Rev 12:3). His robe dipped in blood (19:13) and his declaration that he will tread the winepress of God's wrath (19:15) allude to the image of the divine warrior (Isa 63:1–6). All this indicates that Christ is now the instrument of God's judgment.

Traditionally the armies of heaven were described as made up of angels. The white-dressed army of the King of kings, however, calls to mind the vast multitude of Revelation 7:9–14, thus implying that this army is made up of glorified humans, perhaps martyrs who died for their faith. Therefore, in this scene, the earthly and heavenly conflicts are combined. Those who had suffered earthly persecution now join in the victory of the heavenly realm. The great feast is declared prior to the defeat of the beasts and the armies of the dragon (Rev 19:17b–18). So it is a call not to battle but to the sacrificial feast of the victory over evil.

The mention of the winepress (Rev 19:15b) hearkens back to the harvest of the earth, which was carried out by an angel. It is now the King of kings who treads out the winepress. Aside from the harvest, much of the King of kings imagery (Rev 19:12ff.) recalls the promises made in the messages to the churches (Rev 2—3) (see Fig. 17 below).

In the Old Testament tradition the divine name of God, Yahweh, was spoken only once a year on the Day of Atonement by the high priest in the Holy of Holies. Whatever the name written on

Figure 17

King of Kings Imagery (Rev 19)	Messages to the Churches (Rev 1—3)
"His eyes are like a flame of fire." —Rev 19:12a	*"The Son of God, who has eyes like a flame of fire."*—Rev 2:18
"He has a name inscribed that no one knows but himself." —Rev 19:12b	*"I will give a white stone, and on the white stone is written a new name that no one knows except the one who receives it."*—Rev 2:17b
"From his mouth comes a sharp sword with which to strike down the nations."—Rev 19:15	*"I will come to you soon and make war against them with the sword of my mouth."*—Rev 2:16

the King of kings may be, in Jewish thought and culture a name was believed to contain the essence and the reality of the person to whom it belonged. Speaking the name made the individual somehow present to the one who uttered it; hence the sacredness of the divine name and the mystery of the name written on the King of kings.

On the whole, these verses do not appear to be compatible with the image of the gentle, loving Christ, nor with his teaching to love one's enemies. There is, however, a hope for the punishment of the wicked and the final reward of those who remain faithful in spite of persecution. Further, the punishment of the wicked is consistent with the concern for justice, and it must be noted that it is God who carries it out, not human beings. These verses must be read and interpreted in light of the cosmic battle between good and evil, the heavenly realm and the earthly realm, God and Satan. In the end evil will be totally vanquished.

Revelation 20—The Thousand-Year Reign and the Great Millennium

We now read of the fate of the dragon and a principal origin for the millennial elements of modern apocalyptic expectation. If one is to look sequentially at the Book of Revelation with regard to the millennium, one must note what exactly is described surrounding the thousand-year reign.

1. The dragon, Satan, is chained and hurled into the abyss.
2. Those beheaded for the faith come back to life in the first resurrection.
3. They reign with Christ for a thousand years, *then*
4. The dragon is unleashed.
5. He and the nations attack the beloved city and are defeated by heaven before being hurled into the pool of sulphur.
6. The second resurrection and the Last Judgment occur.

As with the blowing of the fifth trumpet (Rev 9:1), an angel now comes down from heaven with the key to the abyss (in 9:1 it was a star). This angel seizes the dragon and chains him for a thousand years, hurling him into the abyss. This confinement is only temporary, however. Chaos is confined, but not destroyed.

The symbolism recalls the story of creation at the very beginning of the Bible. As God created the world, he confined the abyss—understood to be the sea—and separated it from dry land (Gen 1:9–10). In doing so, God's creative power separated order (land) from chaos (sea, abyss) and the realm of life from that of death. Throughout Revelation, particularly in the second half, all of the principal forces of evil emerge from the sea. In Revelation 12:15 the dragon (serpent) spews a torrent of water from his mouth "to sweep [the woman] away with the flood." However, the earth comes to the woman's rescue, swallowing up the flood. In Revelation 13:1, the first beast emerges from the sea. Now, in Revelation 20, the dragon is confined to the abyss, placing evil with chaos and separating it from goodness, order, and life.

During the time of the dragon's confinement, "those who had been beheaded for their testimony to Jesus and for the word of God" reign with Christ for a thousand years (Rev 20:4). Various elements are interwoven throughout the description of the thousand-year reign, which I discuss individually.

This reign is referred to as the first resurrection (Rev 20:5), enjoyed by those who were faithful to Christ at the cost of their lives. The rest of the dead do not come back to life until the thousand years are over, just prior to the Last Judgment. Throughout Revelation there are visions in which the martyrs stand out above other witnesses to the faith—the fifth seal, the vast multitude dressed in white, the companions of the Lamb. There is a distinction between those who have given their lives for the faith—the martyrs—and those who simply do not. The participants in the first resurrection are yet another example in which Revelation distinguishes those who give the fullest measure of loyalty to Christ, and offers a strong incentive during times of persecution to remain true to the faith, even to the point of death.

The thousand years is seen in comparison to a vision of the two witnesses who suffered death for prophesying and giving witness (Rev 11:2). The period of the witnesses' preaching (1,260 days) and of Gentile occupation and persecution (forty-two months) both come out to three-and-a-half years, an insignificant amount of time compared to a thousand years of triumph.

The martyrs are described as reigning and serving God and Christ as priests (Rev 20:6), which suggests that their roles are as mediators between God and the rest of humanity. The beatitude (Rev 20:6) builds upon the beatitude of the three angels (Rev 14:13): those who die in the Lord share in the first resurrection.

The unleashing of Satan for the final attack includes the images of Gog and Magog from Ezekiel 38—39, which signify all of the pagan nations who are at odds with Christianity (Rev 20:8). This resurgence of evil reflects the ancient view of the cosmos as cyclical, still prevalent at that time in ancient pagan cultures who saw the struggle between good and evil as ongoing and repeatedly renewed (see chapter 1, the section on Apocalyptic Eschatology). In the Book of Revelation, however, the Jewish and Christian belief takes precedence in that the struggle ultimately comes to an end with the powers of evil being vanquished once and for all, "forever and ever" (Rev 20:10b).

Like the other numbers found in the Book of Revelation and other apocalyptic works, terms such as *thousand-year reign* and *thousand* must not be taken literally. Rather, they symbolize the long period of Satan's confinement and the reign of Christ. The saints reign with him in virtue of their baptismal victory; through the sacrament, they entered into the victory of Christ's death and resurrection. The chaining of Satan is symbolic of this victory over death and the forces of evil.

Revelation 20:11–15—The Last Judgment

After Satan has been vanquished once and for all, the second resurrection takes place. Death and the netherworld give up the deceased and they are judged before the throne of God. This image of judgment begins with the vision of the One sitting on a great white throne while the earth and sky flee from his presence. This throne is distinct from the throne of Revelation 4:2 in that it is described specifically as white. After the sea and the netherworld give up the dead, both are cast into the pool of fire, which indicates finality to the destruction of chaos and ultimately of death itself.

The vision depicts universal judgment of the dead and links resurrection with judgment. As this is the second resurrection, as distinct from the first, this judgment does not include those who reigned with Christ for a thousand years—those martyred for their faith. The Last Judgment is upon those whose resurrection takes place after the thousand-year reign.

Revelation 20:11–15 presents two concepts of judgment: the book of life and the heavenly record of deeds.

The **book of life** suggests a revelation to which people are expected to respond. It reminds us that salvation is a gift from God and implies that some are directly called to receive special grace or revelation and either respond to it or deny it. The image of the book of life occurs in both the Hebrew and the Christian Scriptures (Exod 32:32–33; Ps 69:29; Dan 12:1; Mal 3:16; Luke 10:20; Phil 4:3; Heb 12:23) and is spoken of frequently in the Book of Revelation (3:5; 13:8; 17:8; 20:15; 21:27). In the book are written the names of those who are active citizens of the kingdom of God. Those who worship the beast are not included (Rev 13:8).

Although it symbolizes God's grace and free gift of salvation, the book of life still allows for free will. The inclusion of the book of life hearkens back to the message to Sardis. As a reward to the victor, their name is not erased from the book of life (Rev 3:5). Consequently, we are ultimately responsible for what we do, and one's name can be removed from the book.

The **heavenly record of deeds** (Rev 20:12b) forms an explicit link between one's actions and one's salvation. This includes every human being who now comes for judgment.[25] The dead are judged "according to their works, as recorded in the books" (Rev 20:12), rather than according to whether or not they have received revelation. The idea is that God keeps a record of deeds, and that God himself does not judge—rather, human beings, by their actions, write their own judgment.

The "predestination" implied by the book of life is not understood in the Calvinistic sense, in which God has predestined some for salvation and others not. While the book of life indicates that some are destined to hear and respond to the gospel of Christ—those born Christian or those who hear it through evangelization and conversion—others are not. Human freedom to live according to the gospel allows for the existence of the heavenly record as a basis for God's judgment of all the dead, not just those predestined to follow Christ. In Revelation, a book of destiny (book of life) is placed alongside a book of human freedom and responsibility (heavenly record of deeds).

Judgment and salvation, therefore, include both those who receive revelation and those who do not, those destined to hear and respond to the Christian message and those who are not. The book of life, however, suggests a select group (Christians?), while the heavenly record of deeds implies a more universal inclusion (non-Christian people?) whose deeds are the basis of judgment. Hence, the Book of Revelation suggests that salvation is possible outside the faith community of the church.[26]

Revelation 21—22:5—The New Creation

The seventh and last vision is of the new creation and the New Jerusalem. After witnessing the doom of the wicked and the destruction of death and evil, John sees the final culmination of bliss for those who emerged in the second resurrection, were found worthy in the Last Judgment, and survived the second death. This creation of a new heaven and a new earth is consistent with prophetic thought, particularly with prophecies that promoted the ideas of a new Temple, a New Israel, and a new covenant. However, in the apocalyptic mindset, the new heaven and the new earth emerge from the end of the old and provide a new world that lives in harmony with the heavenly realm.

An important statement is the declaration of Revelation 21:5–6. The author is commanded to write down what he sees and hears because "it is done!" or "they are accomplished." John notes that the vision he is about to see has been fulfilled. Therefore one can read these visions in terms of present reality.[27] For the reader of Revelation, the new creation and the New Jerusalem are reflections of the reality that is the church and the reality of a world redeemed by Christ. The old order prior to Christ has passed. In virtue of his death and resurrection, the new order has come, and the church is the source of his grace and presence in the world.

The new heaven and the new earth are first described in negative terms, that is, through the observation that the former heaven and the former earth are gone. But they are then described in a positive light, noting the New Jerusalem. The idea of a New Jerusalem is proposed in the prophets (Isa 54), and would have had particular meaning for the Jews in the period following the city's destruction in AD 70. However, rather than expressing hope for a historical and physical restoration, Revelation expresses the faith that despite the absence of the Temple and the presence of persecution, God is still present and accessible to his people in and through the church (Rev 21:3–4). Revelation 21:9—22:5 describes this vision of the New Jerusalem in greater detail.

In the first verse of the vision John observes that the sea no longer exists (Rev 21:1). In the new creation this coincides with the nonexistence of death (Rev 21:4). Just as Baal conquered Yam, the god of the sea/chaos, Yahweh, in Christ, conquered death, symbolized by the sea. Whereas Baal, after conquering Yam, is swallowed by Mot, the god of death, Christ conquers death. Hence death has no place in the new creation.

Following the oration of verses 3–4, John quotes God for the second time in the Book of Revelation. In both of these quotations (Rev 1:8 and 21:6) God declares himself to be "the Alpha and the Omega." To this second quotation is added "the beginning and the end." God assures fellowship to those who worship him and punishment on those who deny Christ.

To those who thirst, God will give them water from the life-giving spring (Rev 21:6b–7). This is not necessarily an allusion to baptism, but is inspired by Isaiah 55:1: "Ho, everyone who thirsts, come to the waters." The promise of fellowship of Revelation 21:7b—"I will be their God and they will be my children"—recalls 2 Samuel 7:14. To those who are cowards, who deny Christ so as to be safe—to avoid persecution and thereby throw in their lot with idolatry—God promises the fiery pool of the second death (Rev 21:8).

John describes the New Jerusalem in detail. Yet no one can say for certain what exactly the symbolism is meant to represent. The experience of being accompanied by an angel to a high mountain recalls the experience of Ezekiel 40:2 in which the prophet, too, is brought to a high mountain by an angelic being to see the new Temple. The New Jerusalem gleams with the splendor of God

(Rev 21:11). This splendid light is also spoken of by Isaiah (60:1f.) as he describes the glory of the Lord.

The description of the New Jerusalem contrasts with that of the whore of Babylon (Rev 17:1—19:10). Both passages are introduced by an angel who held one of the seven bowls, who calls John to witness the vision. In the vision of Babylon, the angel says: "Come. I will show you the judgment of the great whore" (Rev 17:1). In the vision of the New Jerusalem the angel states: "Come. I will show you the bride, the wife of the Lamb" (Rev 21:9). Hence, both extended visions that follow upon the seven last plagues are meant to present a contrast between the abhorrence of the whore who "rides" the beast and the beauty of the bride who marries the Lamb.

The New Jerusalem is a city of great richness, far surpassing any city or manifestation of the ancient pagan gods. The city and its streets are pure gold, so pure as to be crystal clear (Rev 21:18, 21). The twelve gates are bejeweled with pearls, considered the most valuable stone in the ancient world (Rev 21:21). These gates of pearl become, therefore, a symbol of the great wealth and beauty of the New Jerusalem. The twelve precious stones that adorn the foundation (Rev 21:19–20) correspond to the twelve stones on the breastplate of the high priest, described in Exodus 28:15–21.

The city is Christian, but built upon the old covenant with Israel. John's description of the city's wall and foundations reflects the prophetic background of his vision and its insertion into Christian faith. There are twelve gates on which are written the twelve tribes of Israel and a foundation of twelve courses of stones on which are written the names of the twelve apostles. The placement of the gates and the names of the tribes recall the concluding verses of the Book of Ezekiel (Ezek 48:30). The wall can be seen as the bulwark of faith that protects the saints of God against the evil assault of the world through persecutions.

The city is a manifestation of God's presence. Like Ezekiel John goes into some detail as to the measurement of the city itself. The shape of the city is a perfect square and its measurements are all multiples of the symbolic number 12 (Rev 21:16–17). The city itself is 12,000 furlongs in length and width (21:16). Its wall is 144 cubits (12 x 12) in height. The shape of the city—a perfect cube— symbolizes perfection. This shape occurs frequently in the prophetic visions of the new Temple, the most notable being the shape of the Holy of Holies of Solomon's Temple (1 Kgs 6:20) in which the structure was also cubic. The perfect cube of the Holy of Holies housed the presence of God in the Temple; so the cubic shape of the New Jerusalem manifests the presence of God in the entire city, which symbolizes the church. As God was present with the ark of the covenant residing in the Holy of Holies, so God is now present to and in the church.

The New Jerusalem is a place of great intimacy with God, where "they will see his face" (Rev 22:4a). This was unheard of in Old Testament theology, because it was believed that to see the face of God meant certain death (Exod 33:20). Because of this, to see God face to face was expressed only as a wish (Ps 17:15; 42:2–3). This intimacy is now granted because the barrier between God and humanity has been torn down (Matt 27:51; Mark 15:38; Luke 23:45). We now enjoy a veritable "face-to-face" intimacy with God by virtue of Christ's death and resurrection.

The New Jerusalem does not have a Temple. For a person of Jewish heritage, this concept would be radical if not downright shocking, because the Temple was central to Jewish faith and worship. Within the Temple was the Holy of Holies, where God's presence was the most manifest. It was a room accessible only to the high priest on one day a year—the Day of Atonement. Now, in the New Jerusalem, there is no need for a Temple to house the presence of God. Rather, God is fully present and fully accessible to all of the citizens of the New Jerusalem. Christ is present throughout the church, the people of God. Therefore, there is no need for a specific dwelling for God on earth.

This is consistent with the theology found throughout the New Testament. St. Paul speaks repeatedly of the church as the new Temple, the presence of God. In 1 Corinthians he asks:

> Do you not know that you are God's temple and that God's Spirit dwells in you? If anyone destroys God's temple, God will destroy that person. For God's temple is holy, and you are that temple. (1 Cor 3:16–17)

In the Letter to the Ephesians, Paul speaks of the people within the church as a whole forming the Temple of God:

> You are citizens with the saints and also members of the household of God, built upon the foundation of the apostles and prophets, with Christ Jesus himself as the cornerstone. In him the whole structure is joined together and grows into a holy temple in the Lord; in whom you also are built together spiritually into a dwelling-place for God. (Eph 2:19–22)

Finally, early in the Book of Revelation, the church in Philadelphia is assured that the conqueror will be made "a pillar in the temple of my God; [he] will never go out of it" (Rev 3:12). All of these teachings can be applied to the vision that God himself serves as Temple within the New Jerusalem. That Temple is the church made up of the people of God.

This observation, of course, comes in the years following the destruction of the Temple by the Romans in AD 70. Because of the importance of the Temple its destruction resulted in a crisis with regard to the identity of the Jews and the Jewish converts to Christianity. Can Judaism (or people of Jewish heritage) survive without a Temple? For the Christian faith, Revelation 21:22 provides the answer: the Lord God is the Temple. God's presence is within the people who make up the church. It manifests itself in the close intimacy between God and humanity that has now been achieved through Jesus Christ. Just as there is no further need for heavenly or angelic mediators between God and humanity, because Jesus is now our mediator, so too is there no further need for a Temple. God himself, within the church, serves as the Temple of the New Jerusalem.

The New Jerusalem is a universal city. All people of good will are welcome in the universal church, to walk by the light of the glory of God (Rev 21:24–27; 22:5). Just as the sun and the moon shed light on the entire world—in both the day and the night—so too will God's light and holiness be extended from the confines of a temple to infuse all of creation. The city's gates are never shut (see Isa 60:11), and all the kings of the earth, symbolizing all peoples, may enter to bring the treasures of their devotion and worship to God, and to walk by God's light (see Isa 60:3).

Finally, the New Jerusalem restores the primordial paradise found in the Garden of Eden before the sin of Adam and Eve and restores many times over the paradise of God's original creation. The "river of the water of life" (Rev 22:1), also described in Genesis (2:10–14), reflects the traditional image of a sacred stream flowing from a sacred garden. Ezekiel has a vision of this restoration, in which a stream flowing out from beneath the threshold of the Temple purifies all waters with which it mingles and provides life and sustenance for all creatures (Ezek 47:1–12). In the New Jerusalem the author of Revelation combines the Genesis image with Ezekiel's vision of waters that flow from the throne of God and of the Lamb, thereby symbolizing the life-giving grace that flows from God through the church out to the entire world.

Another symbol drawn from Genesis is the tree of life. In the message to Ephesus (Rev 2:7) the victor is promised food from the tree of life. Whereas in Genesis, there is only one tree of life (Gen 2:9), in Revelation many trees of life spring up "on either side of the river" (Rev 22:2). Fruit is provided twelve times a year, fruit that gives nourishment and healing.

THE END OF THE REVELATION

The epilogue of the Book of Revelation (Rev 22:6–21) is a literary winding down that serves to wrap up the vision portion of the book (vv. 6–9). After this, the format returns to that of a letter to the congregation to whom Revelation is written (vv. 10–22). When the letter concludes the setting returns to liturgy (vv. 17–21), which begins with Christ and the heavenly host, and concludes with John's final address to his listeners. With one last greeting and a call for Christ to come soon, the Book of Revelation draws to a close.

The epilogue summarizes the entire message of the Book of Revelation: to hold fast, worship God alone, endure with patience, and believe in Jesus, who will reward those who endure. Most of the verses of the epilogue repeat verses that occur in other portions throughout the Book of Revelation. It is a densely symbolic summary of the entire message that makes use of symbols that have appeared throughout the book.

The angel assures John that what he reveals is true (Rev 22:6; cf. 1:1). Five times it is declared that the appointed time is "near" or "soon." The single phrase, "I am coming soon," is uttered three times by Christ in the epilogue (Rev 22:7, 12, 20). The angel's assurance that the revelation is true echoes Revelation 19:9. In 22:16, it is made clear that Jesus himself is speaking and has sent the revelation to the churches. The sixth beatitude of the book repeats the first, uttered in the prologue, which declares blessed those who heed the message of this book (Rev 1:3).

The account of John falling down to worship the angelic interpreter, which repeats the account of 19:10 almost verbatim, serves as yet another reminder that worship belongs to God.

In Revelation 22:10 John is given an order to pass along the visions he has witnessed. This order is fulfilled in the writing and the reading of the book itself. The repetition in verse 10b of the words of the prologue, "the time is near" (Rev 1:3b), suggests a sense of urgency.

The words of 22:11 appear to be a kind of surrender to the fact that the wicked are not likely to change their ways. John may have had little hope for the wicked to repent, or perhaps he believed that there was a certain point at which it would be too late to change one's ways. This sentiment is found throughout Scripture. Daniel 12:10 states that "the wicked shall prove wicked." Ezekiel 3:27 says simply, "let him heed who will, and let him resist who will." Even the Gospels acknowledge that some will respond neither to the gospel message nor to God's judgment. The Gospel of Luke states that if people do not listen to Moses and the Prophets "they will not be convinced even if one should rise from the dead" (parable of the rich man and Lazarus—Luke 16:31). John may have had the same feelings toward the wicked, while he continued to urge the faithful to remain virtuous and holy. In the end, God will not force the choice on the people. Either they will remain in their wicked ways, or, as is stated in Revelation 1:3 and 22:7, they will "[keep] the words of the prophecy of this book."

Worship has extended from the One seated on the throne to the Lamb who was slain (Rev 4). Jesus now identifies himself as the

Lamb seated on the throne. All aspects of divine power are now identified in the risen Christ. Jesus now declares himself "the Alpha and the Omega" (cf. Rev 1:8; 21:6), including "the beginning and the end" (cf. Rev 21:6), now adding "the first and the last" (cf. Rev 1:17). This threefold title of "the Alpha and the Omega, the first and the last, the beginning and the end" (Rev 22:13) is a threefold expression of completeness, declaring that the fullness of creation (beginning) and redemption (end) resides in Jesus Christ. (Note the parallel to the threefold completeness found in "Holy, holy, holy.") All worship now belongs to Christ, who with the Father encompasses all time, creation, and authority.

The final beatitude of Revelation (22:14–15) is "blessed are those who wash their robes [cf. Rev 7:14b], so that they will have the right to the tree of life [cf. Rev 2:7] and may enter the city by the gates." The mention of the city gates reinforces the contrast between the blessed—those who are allowed within—and sinners—those who remain outside.

Jesus identifies himself as the source of the revelation, thereby guaranteeing the authenticity of its testimony (Rev 22:16); declares himself the "root and descendant of David," which connects him with the messianic promise given to the king; and identifies himself as the morning star, which symbolizes his messianic authority and victory over death and echoes the promise made to Thyatira in Revelation 2:26f. Finally, the bride (Rev 22:17) is a metaphor not only for the church, but also for the Spirit, which calls humanity to share in the salvation of Jesus Christ. Through that salvation, the Christian community is wedded to Christ. Christ issues his invitation for all to share freely in the waters of his salvation.

To a people still burdened by persecution, Revelation concludes with a final assurance by Jesus that he is coming soon. The people respond with an intercessory prayer, *Maranatha*, calling upon Jesus to come. This prayer has descended through the ages as among the most basic of prayers, encompassing the hope and mystery of the Christian faith. "Christ has died, Christ is risen, Christ will come again" is one of four prayers we pray when proclaiming the mystery of faith during the eucharistic prayer of the Mass. Indeed, Christ will come again, and the constant prayer of the Christian church, echoed through the centuries, serves to conclude the revelation of hope to a persecuted people who long for the Savior to return—*Maranatha!* Come, Lord Jesus!

In the end, it is the grace of the Lord Jesus Christ that is sufficient to sustain Christianity and its people for all time, in all places, in all circumstances. John utters a final benediction, calling upon that grace to be with his listeners, and indeed with all those who read the message of the Book of Revelation. We receive that grace even today as we begin the third millennium of Christianity, and that grace will be with us until Christ comes again.

May that grace continue to animate and invigorate the church in the years and the centuries ahead. May that grace of the Lord Jesus be with all of us who endure in faith, continuing to wait and hope for the day when Christ will return. *Maranatha!* Come, Lord Jesus!

STUDY QUESTIONS

Introduction and Background

1. What is the significance of setting Revelation within the context of worship?
2. Who are the principal characters of Revelation?
3. *When do we receive revelation in our worship?*

Setting the Stage for the Revelation

1. What is the revelation that is the subject of the Book of Revelation?
2. What are some of the titles used for Jesus Christ and God the Father in Revelation 1? What significance do these titles have?
3. *Imagine a letter like the letters to the seven churches being written to you: What praise do you receive? What reproaches?*
4. *What praises or reproaches could be addressed to your parish/diocese/nation?*

The Heavenly Throne Room

1. What are the traditional interpretations for the twenty-four elders and the four living creatures? What are other possible interpretations?
2. What is the significance of the Lamb, as he appears and is worshiped in Revelation 5?
3. *How can we approach our eucharistic liturgy in light of Revelation 4 and 5?*

The Heavenly Intervention

1. What do the four horsemen and sixth trumpet bring about in God's intervention?
2. What do the sixth seal and the first four trumpets bring about?
3. What are possible ways of interpreting the 144,000 and the countless multitude of Revelation 7?
4. What is the lesson of the fifth seal (souls of the martyrs under the altar)?
5. *In what places can you recognize God's intervention in your life and in the life or history of the church?*

The Cosmic Conflict

1. What are the possible meanings behind the woman and dragon of Revelation 12?
2. What is a likely source for the story of the woman and the dragon?
3. If Revelation identifies the dragon as Satan, who might be symbolized in the first beast?
4. What is the meaning behind 666?
5. *Identification of the woman as Mary, although not intended by the author of Revelation, has become part of popular Catholic devotion. How does this image of Mary help your personal devotion to her?*

The Fall of Rome

1. How are the seven bowls reminiscent of the Exodus from Egypt?
2. What is the irony of Armageddon in the Book of Revelation?
3. What is the contrasting image to the whore of Babylon? How does the symbolism relate to the conflict faced by Christians in the late first century?
4. *If "Alleluia" appears at the wedding feast of the Lamb, after the victory over Babylon, what does that imply in our use of "Alleluia" during our own celebration of the Mass?*
5. *If "Alleluia" is only portrayed in the New Testament as part of the liturgy of heaven, how can we therefore understand our liturgy, which also makes use of "Alleluia"?*

The Final Victory and the New Creation

1. What images does Revelation 19 use to depict the victory of the King of kings?
2. How is "predestination" understood in Revelation 20?
3. What does it mean that there will be no sea in the new creation? That the New Jerusalem has no temple?
4. What other images does the author use to describe the New Jerusalem? What do these images signify for us as Christians?
5. *The prayer with which Revelation ends—"Come, Lord Jesus!"— is echoed in the eucharistic acclamation "Christ has died, Christ is risen, Christ will come again." How do this prayer and this acclamation challenge or inspire us to live as Christians?*

EPILOGUE
ARE WE AN APOCALYPTIC PEOPLE?

The simple answer is yes. We are not, however, apocalyptic in the American fundamentalist sense, fixated on the literal fulfillment of a doom prophecy extrapolated from Holy Scripture. While we look for Christ to come again we are not so engrossed in the second coming that we focus more on the future parousia than on the basic call to live and spread the gospel now.

Rather, in the spirit of Daniel and Revelation, we strive to see beyond our experiences as people of faith to the greater reality of the kingdom of God, which Jesus declared is already among us (Luke 17:20–21). Whether it be suffering and persecution, political tensions with our values as church, worship as a community before the altar of eucharistic sacrifice, or renewing ourselves in whatever vocation God has called us to, as apocalyptic people we see our prayer, our struggle, our suffering, and our work as part of the greater dynamic of God's presence and action in our world.

In that vein, do we celebrate our Mass apocalyptically, as a participation in the eternal liturgy of heaven (Rev 4) and a foretaste of the heavenly banquet? If so, do we celebrate it accordingly with full participation and eager anticipation of uniting ourselves to Christ through the Eucharist? "The word of the Lord," "Happy are those who are called to this supper [of the Lamb]."

Do we experience suffering and sickness apocalyptically as a participation in the suffering of Christ for the salvation of souls? If so, how do we see Christ suffering with us, or see Christ present to us? "I want to know Christ and the power of his resurrection and the sharing of his sufferings by becoming like him in his death" (Phil 3:10), "I am now rejoicing in my sufferings for your sake, and in my flesh I am completing what is lacking in Christ's afflictions for the sake of his body, that is, the church" (Col 1:24). "When you

137

saw only one set of footprints, it was then that I carried you" ("Footprints in the Sand").

Do we view the sacrament of matrimony apocalyptically, as truly a symbol of Christ's love for his church? If so, how do we live for each other "in good times and in bad, in sickness and in health...all the days of [our] life"? "Therefore a man leaves his father and his mother and clings to his wife, and they become one flesh" (Gen 2:24); "the marriage of the Lamb has come, and his bride has made herself ready" (Rev 19:7).

Do we see our church apocalyptically as the New Jerusalem (Rev 21) and as the body of Christ, carrying out his work through the ministry of its members? "So we, who are many, are one body in Christ, and individually we are members one of another" (Rom 12:5); "For in the one Spirit we were all baptized into one body" (1 Cor 12:13); "Now you are the body of Christ and individually members of it" (1 Cor 12:27).

Can we view our church's history apocalyptically? If so, how can we understand the good and the bad, the triumphs and tragedies, the sanctity and corruption, the honor and shame of our church throughout history—such as the mass excitement over the election of a new Holy Father, and the shameful humiliation over recent scandal of clergy sexual abuse? "I will ask the Father, and he will give you another Advocate, to be with you forever" (John 14:16); "Remember, I am with you always, to the end of the age" (Matt 28:20).

How can we understand the church's experience of persecution, or fourteenth-century Europe's experience of the Black Death pandemic, the poverty of the Great Depression, and the horror of the Nazi Holocaust through the lens of Christian faith in a loving God? Can we retell the events of September 11, 2001, so as to emphasize God's unwavering and loving presence, and even God's will and intervention throughout such a devastating event?

This is what the authors of Daniel and Revelation sought to accomplish in the midst of suffering and persecution. This is what St. Paul sought to accomplish as the early Christians faced the reality of dying before Jesus came again (1 and 2 Thess). This is what the evangelists sought to do in relating the words of Christ in light of past and imminent catastrophe, all with the basic message that one should be steadfast in faith and in bearing witness to Christ regardless of what may come.

As apocalyptic people we too see the world differently through the eyes of faith. We see a world sanctified by the death and resurrection of Christ. We see a world in which God is very much present to his people. Therefore, we are not discouraged by the presence and action of evil.

NOTES

1. AN INTRODUCTION TO APOCALYPTIC LITERATURE

What Do We Mean by "Apocalyptic" Literature?

1. John J. Collins, ed., *Apocalypse: The Morphology of a Genre, Semeia* 14 (Atlanta, GA: The Society of Biblical Literature, 1979), 9.

2. Genesis 49:1–27—Jacob's last words are an example of a testament in which he utters oracles regarding the development of the tribes of Israel from the families of his twelve sons.

3. Dorothy Jonaitis, *Unmasking Apocalyptic Texts: A Guide to Preaching and Teaching* (New York/Mahwah, NJ: Paulist Press, 2005), 11–12.

Apocalyptic Eschatology

4. James H. Charlesworth, ed., *The Old Testament Pseudepigrapha*, vol. 1: *Apocalyptic Literature and Testaments* (New York: Doubleday, 1983), 156.

5. Interpreted through Christian eyes, the eighth "day" would also correspond to the Lord's day (Sunday), the day after the seventh (or Sabbath) day.

6. Alexander Roberts, DD, and James Donaldson, LLD, eds., *The Ante-Nicene Fathers: Translations of the Writings of the Fathers Down to A.D. 325* (Grand Rapids, MI: Eerdmans, 1979), I: 239.

7. Raymond E. Brown, SS, *An Introduction to the New Testament* (New York: Doubleday, 1997), 802.

The Books of Enoch

8. Charlesworth, *The Old Testament Pseudepigrapha*, 6.

9. Roberts and Donaldson, *The Ante-Nicene Fathers*, IV: 15.
10. Ibid., III: 362.
11. Charlesworth, *The Old Testament Pseudepigrapha*, 5.
12. Ibid., 32.

2. APOCALYPTIC PROPHECY

1. See also the development and victory of Gideon's army in Judges 7.

3. THE BOOK OF DANIEL

Background

1. John J. Collins, *Old Testament Message*, vol. 15: *Daniel, First Maccabees, Second Maccabees* (Wilmington, DE: Michael Glazier, 1981), 3.
2. Scott M. Lewis, SJ, *What Are They Saying about New Testament Apocalyptic?* (New York/Mahwah, NJ: Paulist Press, 2004), 56–57.
3. Neil J. McEleney, CSP, "1–2 Maccabees," in *The New Jerome Biblical Commentary*, ed. R. E. Brown, SS, et al. (Englewood Cliffs, NJ: Prentice Hall, 1990), 426.
4. Collins, *Old Testament Message*, 1–2.
5. S. H. Hooke, *Middle Eastern Mythology* (New York: Penguin Putnam, 1963), 90.
6. Raymond E. Brown, SS, and Raymond F. Collins, "Canonicity," in *The New Jerome Biblical Commentary*, 1038.

The Message of Daniel

7. Collins, *Old Testament Message*, 52–53.
8. Louis F. Hartman, CSsR, and Alexander A. Di Lella, OFM, "Daniel," in *The New Jerome Biblical Commentary*, 414–15.
9. Ibid., 416–17.

4. APOCALYPTIC THEMES IN THE NEW TESTAMENT

Judgment and the Second Coming of Christ

1. This would mean that the narrative formula of the Last Supper was put in writing first by Paul (1 Cor 13:17–34) around AD 54 before Mark incorporated a similar narration in his Gospel (Mark 14:22–24).

2. Joseph T. Kelly, *101 Questions and Answers on the Four Last Things* (New York/Mahwah, NJ: Paulist Press, 2006), 49.

3. Matthew also hints at the end times with the parable of the wedding banquet (Matt 22:1–14) and the questions regarding resurrection (Matt 22:23–33).

4. Kelly, *101 Questions and Answers on the Four Last Things*, 48.

5. THE BOOK OF REVELATION

Introduction and Background

1. Matthew 24:36, Mark 13:32, and reiterated in Acts 1:6–7.

2. Joseph T. Kelly, *101 Questions and Answers on the Four Last Things* (New York/Mahwah, NJ: Paulist Press, 2006), 50.

3. Richard E. Whitaker, *The Eerdmans Analytical Concordance to the Revised Standard Version of the Bible* (Grand Rapids, MI: Eerdmans, 1988), 205.

4. Raymond E. Brown, SS, *An Introduction to the New Testament* (New York: Doubleday, 1997), 782.

Setting the Stage for the Revelation

5. William Barclay, *The Daily Study Bible Series: The Revelation of John*, vol. 1 (Philadelphia: Westminster Press, 1976), 31.

6. Adela Yarbro Collins, "The Apocalypse (Revelation)," in *The New Jerome Biblical Commentary*, 1001.

7. Ibid.

The Heavenly Throne Room

8. Ibid., 1004.

The Heavenly Intervention

9. Joel 4:15a in some biblical editions.

10. Adela Yarbro Collins, *The Apocalypse: New Testament Message* 22 (Collegeville, MN: Liturgical Press, 1979), 52.

11. As Dan held land in the northernmost border of the Promised Land, it would have been the first to fall to the enemies descending from the north.

12. Alexander Roberts, DD, and James Donaldson, LLD, eds., *The Ante-Nicene Fathers: Translations of the Writings of the Fathers down to A.D. 325* (Grand Rapids, MI: Eerdmans, 1979), V: 207.

13. Brown, *Introduction to the New Testament*, 181–88.

14. In Revelation 20:1–3 an angel emerges with the key to the abyss and seals Satan within it for a thousand years.

15. Sodom and Gomorrah are especially named in relation to Israel's immorality in Isaiah 1:9–10.

The Cosmic Conflict

16. Wilfrid J. Harrington, OP, "Revelation," in *Sacra Pagina Series*, vol. 16, ed. Daniel J. Harrington, SJ (Collegeville, MN: Liturgical Press, 1993), 129.

17. The prophet Hosea builds upon this image in his own marriage to the unfaithful Gomer. Gomer's infidelity to Hosea parallels Israel's infidelity to Yahweh.

18. Barclay, *The Daily Study Bible Series*, 99.

19. David E. Aune, "Revelation 6—16," *Word Biblical Commentary*, vol. 52b, ed. Bruce M. Metzger et al. (Nashville: Thomas Nelson Publishers, 1998), 770.

20. Patrick W. Skehan, "King of Kings, Lord of Lords (Apoc. 19:16)," *Catholic Biblical Quarterly* 10 (1948): 398.

21. 1 Enoch 7:1; 9:8; 15:1–7.

22. Joel 3:13 in some biblical editions.

The Fall of Rome

23. Isaiah 21:9 is quoted twice in Revelation (14:8; 18:2).

24. Psalms 106, 111—14, 116—18, 135—36, 146, 148—50.

The Final Victory and the New Creation

25. Harrington, "Revelation," 203.
26. A. Y. Collins, *The Apocalypse*, 143.
27. Harrington, "Revelation," 208.

FOR FURTHER READING

Beker, J. Christian. *Paul's Apocalyptic Gospel: The Coming Triumph of God.* Philadelphia: Fortress Press, 1982.

Bellitto, Christopher. *What Every Catholic Should Know about the Millennium.* Liguori, MO: Liguori Publications, 1998.

Brown, Raymond E., SS. *An Introduction to the New Testament.* New York: Doubleday, 1997.

Brown, Raymond E., SS, et al., eds. *The New Jerome Biblical Commentary.* Englewood Cliffs, NJ: Prentice Hall, 1990. See especially Adela Yarbro Collins, "The Apocalypse (Revelation)," 996–1016; Louis F. Hartman, CSsR, and Alexander A. Di Lella, OFM, "Daniel," 406–20; Neil J. McEleney, CSP, "1–2 Maccabees," 421–46.

Charlesworth, James H., ed. *The Old Testament Pseudepigrapha*, vol. 1: *Apocalyptic Literature and Testaments.* New York: Doubleday, 1983.

Collins, John J. *The Apocalyptic Imagination: An Introduction to Jewish Apocalyptic Literature.* Grand Rapids, MI: Eerdmans, 1998.

Collins, John J., ed. *Apocalypse: The Morphology of a Genre. Semeia* 14. Atlanta, GA: The Society of Biblical Literature, 1979.

Decock, Paul B. "Some Issues in Apocalyptic in the Exegetical Literature of the Last Ten Years." *Neotestamentica* 33, no. 1 (1999).

Harrington, Wilfrid. *Understanding the Apocalypse.* Washington: Corpus Cooks, 1969.

Hayes, Zachary, OFM. *Visions of a Future: A Study of Christian Eschatology.* New Theology Studies 8. Collegeville, MN: Liturgical Press, 1992.

Hayes, Zachary. *What Are They Saying about the End of the World?* New York/Mahwah, NJ: Paulist Press, 1983.

Jonaitis, Dorothy. *Unmasking Apocalyptic Texts: A Guide to Preaching and Teaching.* New York/Mahwah, NJ: Paulist Press, 2005.

Kelly, Joseph T. *101 Questions and Answers on the Four Last Things.* New York/Mahwah, NJ: Paulist Press, 2006.

Lewis, Scott M., SJ. *What Are They Saying about New Testament Apocalyptic?* New York/Mahwah, NJ: Paulist Press, 2004.

Matthews, Victor H., and Don C. Benjamin. *Old Testament Parallels: Laws and Stories from the Ancient Near East.* Fully revised and expanded 3rd ed. New York/Mahwah, NJ: Paulist Press, 2006.

Peters, Tiemo Rainer, and Claus Urban, eds. *End of Time: The Provocation of Talking about God.* New York/Mahwah, NJ: Paulist Press, 2004.

Ralph, Margaret Nutting. *The Bible and the End of the World: Should We Be Afraid?* New York/Mahwah, NJ: Paulist Press, 1997.

Stackhouse, Reginald. *The End of the World? A New Look at an Old Belief.* New York/Mahwah, NJ: Paulist Press, 1997.

ON THE BOOK OF REVELATION

Barclay, William. *The Daily Study Bible Series: The Revelation of John,* vol. 1. Philadelphia: Westminster Press, 1976.

Bauckham, Richard. *The Theology of the Book of Revelation.* Cambridge: Cambridge University Press, 1993.

Beale, G. K. *The Book of Revelation.* The New International Greek Testament Commentary. Grand Rapids, MI: Eerdmans, 1999.

Boring, M. Eugene. *Revelation: Interpretation.* Louisville: John Knox Press, 1989.

Collins, Adela Yarbro. *The Apocalypse: New Testament Message 22.* Collegeville, MN: Liturgical Press, 1979.

Collins, Adela Yarbro. *The Combat Myth in the Book of Revelation.* Missoula, MT: Scholars Press, 1976.

Collins, Adela Yarbro. *Crisis and Catharsis: The Power of the Apocalypse.* Philadelphia: Westminster Press, 1984.

Court, John M. *Myth and History in the Book of Revelation.* Atlanta: John Knox Press; London: S.P.C.K., 1979.

Court, John M. *Revelation*. Sheffield, England: Sheffield Academic Press, 1994.

Faley, Roland J. *Apocalypse Then and Now: A Companion to the Book of Revelation*. New York/Mahwah, NJ: Paulist Press, 1999.

Harrington, Wilfrid J., OP. "Revelation." In *Sacra Pagina Series*, vol. 16. Edited by Daniel J. Harrington, SJ. Collegeville, MN: Liturgical Press, 1993.

Malina, Bruce J. *The New Jerusalem in the Revelation of John: The City as Symbol of Life With God*. Collegeville, MN: Liturgical Press, 1995.

ON THE BOOK OF DANIEL

Clifford, Richard J. *The Book of Daniel*. Herald Biblical Booklets. Chicago: Franciscan Herald Press, 1980.

Collins, John J. *The Apocalyptic Vision of the Book of Daniel*. Harvard Semitic Monographs 16. Chico, CA: Scholars Press, 1977.

Collins, John J. *Daniel: A Commentary on the Book of Daniel*. Hermeneia. Minneapolis: Fortress Press, 1993.

Collins, John J. *Old Testament Message*, vol. 15: *Daniel, First Maccabees, Second Maccabees*. Wilmington, DE: Michael Glazier, 1981.

Harrington, Daniel J. *The Maccabean Revolt*. Wilmington, DE: Michael Glazier, 1988.

Hengel, Martin. *Judaism and Hellenism*. 2 vols. Philadelphia: Fortress Press, 1974.

LaCocque, André. *The Book of Daniel*. Atlanta: John Knox Press; London: S.P.C.K., 1979.

Montgomery, J. A. *Daniel*. International Critical Commentary. New York: Scribner's; Edinburgh: T. & T. Clarke, 1927.

Tcherikover, Victor. *Hellenistic Civilization and the Jews*. New York: Atheneum, 1959.

FOR MORE SCHOLARLY STUDIES

Aune, David E. "Revelation." In *Word Biblical Commentary*, vol. 52. Edited by Bruce M. Metzger et al. Nashville: Thomas Nelson Publishers, 1998.

Whitaker, Richard E. *The Eerdmans Analytical Concordance to the Revised Standard Version of the Bible*. Grand Rapids, MI: Eerdmans, 1988.

ON ANCIENT MYTHOLOGY

Hooke, S. H. *Middle Eastern Mythology*. New York: Penguin Putnam, 1963.

INDEX

Heavenly realm, 2, 14, 73, 79,
80–81, 83, 84, 85, 87, 100,
104, 107, 110, 120, 121,
122, 126; heavenly throne
room, 67, 68, 78–82, 95
Hebrew Scriptures, 37, 53,
125
Hebrews (people), 33, 80
Hebrews, Letter to, 55–59
Hell, 4, 14, 78–79
Hellenistic, 13, 36, 37, 38, 41,
42, 44, 52, 56
History, ix–x, xii, 5, 6–7, 9, 11,
12, 15, 17–18, 29, 38, 41,
43, 44, 48, 51, 65, 74,
113, 138; of Christianity,
ix, 11, 66; Jewish/Hebrew,
13, 20–23, 35, 36–38,
41–42, 43, 76–77, 114;
theology of, 35, 41, 48, 52
Holy Spirit, 12, 56, 70–71, 73,
108
Hosea, Book of, 20, 118, 143

Idol/idolatry, 43, *43*, 45, 47, 52,
67, 76, 79, 88, 89, 92,
108, 111, 127
Isaiah, Book of, 23, 24, *25*, 27,
29–31, 71, 73, 77, 83, 87,
107, 108, 117, 121, 127,
128, 130, 131
Ishmael (Palestinian rabbi),
ascension of, 14

Jacob, 17, 77, 83, 88, 89, 101,
140; death of, 83
James, Letter of, 53
Jehu (king of Israel), 20

Jeremiah, Book of, 22, 50–51,
89, 92, 108, 117, 118
Jerusalem, 7, 9, 20, 22, 26, 27,
31, 33, 36, 37, 41, 46, 59,
60, 61, 62, 65–66, 85, 89,
96, 108, 114. *See also*
New Jerusalem
Jesus Christ, 49, 54, 55, 56, 58,
64, 71, 73, 97, 101, 130,
133, 134; death of, 5, 8,
56, 57, 115, 124, 126,
129, 137, 139
Job (person), 39
Job, Book of, 104
Joel, Book of, 23, 24, 87, 93,
109, 143
John, the apostle, 65
John the Baptist, 28
"John," of the Book of
Revelation, 3, 65
John, Gospel of, 65, 71, 82, 138
John, Letters of, 53–54
John, the seer, 96
John Paul II, Pope, 12
Jonah, Book of, 24
Judaism, 22, 23, 37, 41, 48, 66,
130
Jude, Letter of, 54
Judges, the, 18
Judges, Book of, 114, 141
Judgment, 4, 7, 8, 10, 11,
16–17, 18, 24, 28, 29, 39,
46, 53–63, 78, 85–87, 90,
93, 99, 100, 109–13, 119,
120–21, 128, 132; Day of
Judgment, 7, 11; Last
Judgment, 122, 123,
124–26

Justice, 52, 87, 90, 110, 111, 122; social justice, 110
Justin Martyr, Saint, 9

Kingdom(s): on Earth, ix, 11, 24, 79, 83, 112; after the Exile, *43*, 44–45, 48–49, 51; of God, ix, 5, *43*, 45, 72, 99, 125, 137; of Heaven, 53, 60; of Israel, 7, 20, 22, 24, 29, 50, 53; Northern Kingdom (Israel), 20–22, 76, 89; Southern Kingdom (Judah), 20–22, 36, 89
Kings, First Book of, 25, 129
Knowledge, 38, 44, 71, 76, 112

Lament/lamentation, 50, 85–86, 94, 117–18
Lamentations, Book of, 39
Lateran Council, Fifth, 11–12
Latin, 15, 26. *See also* Mass
Law, 28, 29, 47, 49; God's, 47; Mosaic, 28, 29, 53; natural, 30; and order, ix, x; and the Prophets, 22, 28, 39, 97; of righteousness, 17
Lawlessness, 59
Leto, 102, *103*
Leviticus, Book of, 112
Lord Jesus, 55, 56, 58–59, 134
Love, ix, 78, 86–87, 118, 122, 138
Luke, Gospel of, 11, 29, 30, 55, 59–63, 71, 82, 86, 87, 97, 112, 118, 125, 129, 132, 137

Maccabees: Book of, 35; dynasty of (Hasmonean), 38; First Maccabees, 37; Second Maccabees, 37; revolt of, 17, 18, 35, 38
Malachi, Book of, 23, 24, 28–29, 125
Mark, Gospel of, 11, 29, 55, 59–63, 71, 82, 86, 87, 97, 129
Marriage, 70, 118, 138
Martyrs, 9, 12, 69, 78, 85–86, 90, 91, 94, 107, 110, 116, 121, 123–24, 125
Mary, assumption of, 103
Mass, 26, 133, 137
Matthew, Gospel of, 11, 27, 28, 29, 55, 59–63, 71, 78, 82, 86, 87, 97, 102, 112, 129, 138
Megiddo, 113–14
Millenarianism, 8–12
Millennium, x, 8–12, 134
Moses, 28–29, 55, 97, 110, 132; "assumption of," 55
Mot (god of death), 25, 29–31, 127
Mystery, xi, 62, 122, 133
Mystery of Faith, 133
Mythology, 14, 32, 101
   Babylonian, 80, 101
   Canaanite, 24, 25, 31, 39, 71
   Greek, 102